THE

THE CRUCIFIED IS NO STRANGER

SEBASTIAN MOORE

DARTON, LONGMAN & TODD LTD

248·4

First published in Great Britain in 1977 by
Darton, Longman & Todd Ltd
89 Lillie Road, London, SW6 1UD

Copyright © Sebastian Moore, 1977

ISBN 0 232 51375 9

Printed in Great Britain by The Anchor Press Ltd
and bound by Wm Brendon & Son Ltd
both of Tiptree, Essex

Reprinted 1978

Quotations from THE FAMILY REUNION and
COLLECTED POEMS 1909–1962 by T. S. Eliot
are reprinted by permission from Faber and Faber
Ltd and Harcourt, Brace Jovanovich Inc. The poem
From a Norman· Crucifix of 1632 by Charles Causley is
reprinted with permission from Macmillan Ltd., and
quotations from the poems of Robert Frost by permission from Jonathan Cape and Holt, Rinehart &
Winston Inc.

CONTENTS

Part Three
IN PRACTICE

I am the great sun, but you do not see me
I am your husband, but you turn away
I am the captive, but you do not free me
I am the captain you will not obey

I am the truth, but you will not believe me
I am the city, where you will not stay
I am your wife, your child, but you will leave me
I am the God to whom you will not pray

I am your counsel, but you do not hear me
I am the lover whom you will betray
I am the victor, but you do not cheer me
I am the holy dove whom you will slay

I am your life, but if you will not name me
Seal up your soul with tears and never blame me

'From a Norman Crucifix of 1632'
by Charles Causley

INTRODUCTION

I want to say how this book came to be written. For many years I have had a special concern with Christology. I have always had a pressing sense of the *contrast* between Jesus and culture. I felt that this contrast was always being blurred by theologians, by piety, by all the Christian worlds of discourse. It seemed that we were all having it both ways: worshipping a Jesus who at once turns the world upside down and takes his place within it, still the old way up.

Latterly I have felt especially drawn to those few courageous men and women whose commitment to Jesus set them at odds with society and its norms and expectations. It was in such confrontations that a new Christology would be born, a newly marked Christology of contrast.

Contrast. It gave to Jesus many names in my thinking, some named, some only implied: challenge, questioner, question, outsider, prophet, poet, revolutionary, protest.

Recently I began to see that the great contrast between Jesus and normality, that I had for so long felt in my bones, gave to him a more mysterious name that I had been *resisting* in my bones: the name of victim. Everything changed.

I remembered how, long ago, I had wandered with some friends into a country church near Rome. It was the feast of the Sacred Heart, and they were singing the first anthem of Vespers. 'One of the soldiers opened his side with a spear, and immediately there came out blood and water.' Quietly, and with a part of the mind that does not wrestle with concepts, I knew that the whole thing was there: the act of aggression, of sin, releasing the waters of grace. This holistic vision, this symbolic concentration of truth, I experienced and was nourished by – and promptly forgot. For nearly fifteen years.

With the realization that Jesus had to be seen above all as victim, the cumbersome work of the intellect caught up with, and became caught up in, that moment in the country church. For the intellectual work was not denied but deepened. That affair of man with

Jesus, of man-in-society with this new possibility of man, was at its centre a confrontation of bitterness, of sorrow, and of healing. And it was a healing of the mind when the traditional language – 'done to death for our sins' – came at me in a new way: no longer as some sort of transposed application to 'the Christ-event' of a primitive idea of expiation, but as the meaning of the contrast between Jesus and culture. In my thinking, the language of Jesus as the saving victim rose from the dead – and so did my Christian mind.

The most important concept to revive in me was the concept of sin which, like the concept of victim, now came to me in the context of the vision of man that I had been building up over the years. I began to see, at the heart of, and as the explanation of, the whole complex human phenomenon, an unconscious refusal, a failure of man to come to some great meeting-place, a stopping-short. And though at its root unconscious, it was a very powerful refusal, a refusal powered by a nameless and pervasive fear. A refusal so powerful, so influential of all behaviour, so unreachable in its roots, that even the fear that powers it seldom goes by that name.

'What is it that we are refusing?' was the next question. What we are refusing is not, directly at least, 'obedience to God' but some fulness of life to which God is impelling us and which our whole being dreads. Some unbearable personhood, identity, freedom, whose demands beat on our comfortable anonymity and choice of death. Further, something that at root we *are*, a self that is ours yet persistently ignored in favor of the readily satisfiable needs of the ego.

Then there began to emerge an idea that would prove to be the linch-pin. What if Jesus were the representative, the symbol, the embodiment, of this dreaded yet desired self of each of us, this destiny of being human, this unbearable identity and freedom (freedom and identity being really the same thing)? The crucifixion of Jesus then becomes the central drama of man's refusal of his true self. Further, this drama could be seen in two successive situations. First, in its historical incidence, in which it expresses only the *conflict* between normal humanity as handled by the Caiaphases and the Pilates, and the true being of man. Secondly, and much more importantly, in the experience of the believer, who, confronted with Jesus crucified, finds all the evil in his life becoming *explicit* as the wilful destruction of his true self now concrete for him in the man on the cross. And evil made totally explicit is resolved in the forgiveness of God of which the crucifixion thus becomes the symbol and sacrament. All symbols transform. *This* symbol transforms evil into sin and sin into sorrow and forgiveness. And through this conversion the believer finds as his own that identity which first he rejected and crucified. He passes – and we are forever passing, back and forth – from 'crucifying the Lord of glory' to being 'nailed to the cross with Christ'.

The crucified as a symbol that transforms evil into sin and sin into grace: here surely is the intellectual structure of that vision of the soldier's spear opening the side and releasing the torrent of new life.

This structure illuminates Paul's grand idea in Romans, of sin as *explicit* refusal of God in the *myth* of Adam, as operating *clandestinely* and all-pervasively in *history* (the 'culture' of which Jesus has to be victim), as imperfectly explicit through the Law, and finally as totally explicit, and so resolved in the love of God, in the crucifixion. I knew that I was understanding for the first time the statement 'him that knew no sin, God made sin for us that we might become the righteousness of God in him.'

Next, Ernest Becker's book 'The Denial of Death' uncovered for me the roots of that human evil of which the cross is the dramatization and resolution. That those roots lie deep was well-known to Paul. He knew that the evil with which the cross has principally to do lies far beyond what we normally experience as sin, beyond the area that we think of as free choice. Becker showed me that the root is in the very constitution of man as that evolutionarily bizarre phenomenon, the conscious animal: the animal who, *knowing* his total contingency, turns from it in fear and builds the idolatrous image of himself. The root of all human evil, says Becker, is the necessary attempt of man to deny his creaturehood. Here was the validation, amazingly simple yet at great depth, of that sense of the human as less than human, of that subhumanity of culture, that had fascinated me for a decade and that was basic to my understanding of Jesus. Here was anthropological justification for the Christian insight that the evil with which God deals in Christ is necessary, a necessary stage in a process of which God is the meaning. And here, in the poignant picture of the conscious and so fearful animal, was the *anthropology* of my idea of God giving man a destiny he could not take and only comes into in a glorious mystery of blood, sorrow, forgiveness, and rebirth.

I then considered the crucifixion's resolution of our evil in terms of the symbolism that our evil confers upon death. Our egoistic self-importance leads us to see death, which is in reality simply part of the life process, as the end of what we consider as alone significant, the works of the ego. The death of Jesus, the man without sin, shatters this tragic symbolism and reveals a deeper meaning in death – 'return to the Father.' Thus the primary exercise in which the converted consciousness firms itself up is the celebration of the death of the Lord as return to the Father. We affirm our Christian freedom by a rite that flouts our sinful tragic cultural vision of death.

Finally, as I lived with this new vision of the crucified, as I prayed it and shared it, I came to see that it contains a whole ascetico-mystical programme. The art of contemplating Jesus crucified is to come to understand, in painful situations, that the cross that I always first experience as 'life's crucifixion of me' is in reality my crucifixion of life, in other words the Jesus-cross. There is only one true cross, to which all our 'crosses' have to be conformed: and this involves not just asking him to help me carry mine, but *inverting* mine – inverting the roles of crucifier and crucified – to conform to his. The question 'who is crucifying whom? what is crucifying what?', asked prayerfully and reflectively, is, I find, a talisman for liberating my friends from my tyranny and liberating myself from this tyranny.

And now, in a way, you have read this book! But the main ideas are for the individual to grasp imaginatively. And this the reader will be more able to do by following me in the process of their unearthing.

Moreover, this book is based on my own experience. How much I have allowed my ego to try to persuade you of its truth by making it more tidy and watertight than direct experience ever is or needs to be, I do not know. Therefore I stress that it is only a series of hints, not a system of theology to be taken over lock, stock and barrel. I am sure that you will come up with your own, and therefore other, psychic processes in this field, and these are what the book is designed to elicit. In the spiritual life, the only motivational and inertia-shifting insights, the only ones that touch us in our indolence and so make a permanent difference to our lives, are those that have come from ourselves alone, discoveries. Bon voyage therefore!

One last point. This book would not have been possible without some 'revelations' which occurred between myself and some others with whom I worked through the Exercises of Ignatius in the role of 'director'. I am eternally grateful to them for what they have shown me of God's ways with men and women in the mystery of Jesus Christ.

Part One

THE CRUCIFIED

1 THE WORST AND THE BEST

No man can say where evil has its origin in him. That is of the essence of evil. And because the *origin* of evil is lost to us, correspondingly obscure to us is the significance of death. Evil is confused, for us, alike in its beginning and in its end.

The crucifixion of Jesus raises this elusive reality called evil to consciousness. In place of the death in which evil *issues,* there is a death that it *causes*. And he who contemplates this event with the vision of faith feels coming to consciousness within him the origin of evil. And by an extraordinary paradox, his first real conviction that God loves him takes place in the context of his self-discovery as a crucifier.

The crucifixion of Jesus dramatizes that in us which is of its nature faceless. Evil is of its nature diffused. It is in the whole human situation. It is in the crucifiers and in the crucified. In *this* crucifixion, however, there are significant changes. (a) *All* men, the weak as well as the strong, show up as crucifiers, (b) there is *not* evil in the crucified, (c) thus *all* the evil is in the crucifiers, and (d), most difficult to grasp, the evil thus restricted to the crucifiers becomes an *act*, arising in the human heart and proceeding to its destructive conclusion: an *act,* don't you see, and no longer an *atmosphere*. The evil which we experience as a *climate* to which we contribute, becomes, in this august confrontation with the sinless one crucified, a personal act, a source. The spring of evil becomes conscious and personal in face of the Crucified, as we know our worst, and know, for the first time, a total acceptance.

The crucifixion of Jesus makes to be *at man's hands* that death which is rather man's *climate*. That which we kill, in ourselves and in each other, in vicarious and clandestine ways, we have killed once clearly and in the light of day. And death, which is normally a *symbol* of evil, becomes, in this extraordinary instance, evil's *visible effect*.

And *this* is the manifestation of God's love: that extraordinary love that highlights our evil in order to leave us in no doubt that it is accepted.

It is because, in accord with the deepest logic of the psyche, *love* is experienced in the vision of the Crucified: it is because this law of direct ratio between the extent of evil's acting-out and the credibility of the accepting love has been obeyed to the uttermost limits, that the psyche has experienced the plunging of the spear into Christ's side *as* the opening-up of the well-spring of new life.

2 INCARNATION

Christ is our way to God. We go to the Father through him. These propositions have been translated into a rule for meditation: the believer should learn first to fix his eye on Christ, so as to be led, in God's time, to the Father.

Experience, my own and others', has taught me that there is another way. This consists in first becoming convinced of God's love as an all-penetrating force: then coming to experience evil in myself as a reality so pervasive and elusive as to its origin, that I cannot experience *it* as accepted by God in love without the presence of some other factor, in which God's love would *go to meet* my evil. This other factor is the crucifixion and death of Jesus, when this is regarded precisely as 'authorised' by God to declare his love for us. For in this conception, God obeys the deepest psychological law of acceptance: to be convinced of my acceptance, I must know that I am accepted at my worst. God shows me to myself as worse than I had ever conceived – a crucifier of the sinless one – in order to leave in me no possible room for doubt – that is to say no possible *further* experience of evil that might create doubt – that he loves and accepts me.

This imputation of a motive to God for his choice of the cross as revelatory medium is something of an impertinence. It is perhaps the most rational way of pointing to something that is not rational: namely, why God chose the crucifixion of Jesus in its indivisible totality of crucifiers and crucified, and did not merely 'draw good' out of the 'antecedently' not-intended evil that brought the sinless one to the cross. But this idea is only a pointer. In reality the crucifixion of Jesus stands for a meeting between God and evil that is far beyond our rational grasp and is made known to mystics in those moments of irresponsible love that subvert all normal values.

This way of experiencing Christ as the manifestation of God does

4

not go from Christ to God, but from God to Christ. More precisely, from 'God' to 'God in the final absurd fact of us', from God generically to God in the ultimate human specific. Here Christ appears not to the gaze of our innocence: his image clears only as our roots in evil are laid bare, when the cost and shape of really believing in a divine lover of men begin to reveal themselves. There follow three considerations.

1. From this new standpoint, the deficiency of the more usual way reveals itself. Standard meditation-techniques insist that this man I am contemplating died for me. But this shattering truth is revealed only with the appearance of Christ as God's sign of his acceptance of evil. It is seriously distorted when, transplanted from this dark and fertile spiritual soil, it is made to declare itself in the daylight world of our normal relations. There's John who got you that good job – and there's Jesus who died for you.

2. If ever there was a man who went this way, that man was Paul. Paul never knew Jesus. But he knew the spiritual man's wrestle with sin, and he resisted with everything that was in him the notion of a God who would undercut this struggle by an all-embracing love. He heard the words 'it is hard for you to kick against the goad.'

Paul's extreme statements in Romans reflect this vision in which sin dictates the shape of God's love on earth. 'Him that knew no sin, God made sin for us that we might become the righteousness of God in him.' Only with our sin could God touch us sinners. Only in its form, so inalienably ours, could he appear as our familiar. 'God made him sin'. We have been content to describe this phrase as metaphorical, as an extreme way of putting a truth that lies beyond it. In fact, this statement is not a metaphor but a direct transcript of the *divine use of sin,* and as such is a figure that *contains* the truth. But this truth is essentially something experienced thus 'God – sin – Christ – love! The logic of deep human self-awareness is a logic all its own. It is the creation of a new *space,* with the attendant rule that everything that is to become definitive for us does so by occupying that space. The space is marked 'sin'. So *there,* and *that,* God's representative has to be. Christ is there. Christ is that. This way of thinking is only barbarous for the reason.

3. In this way, the mystery of the Incarnation is not the imaginable descent of the God into the womb of the Virgin, but rather comes upon us as a being of God in us. The difficulty of the Incarnation is

5

not in the dogmatic realm. It is the difficulty in a commanded self--acceptance that goes far beyond our limits of self-acceptance. It is the mystery of a God who comes upon us and loves us beyond the limits of our ego-organized potential.

Christ is our way to the Father only because he is the Father's way to us, the Father's way with us, the mysterious expiation of our sin.

When we say, with the Christmas Preface, 'that through knowing God visibly we may be brought to the love of things invisible', we have to ask: what is made visible in Christ? What is made visible is God's touch in the innermost region of the soul where sin qualifies the old man. And this is the divinity of Christ: for only God can touch us there. He touches us by inundating us in a mystery of Incarnation, Passion, Death and Resurrection.

Man is an incurable optimist. He is impelled to improve on his situation, to 'think positively'. In this positive thinking he comes upon a God who loves him and who will be his ally in the struggle with his inner chaos. But the God who loves him is and will remain the projection of his optimism until he is somehow brought by God to turn about and face the chaos and — far more than this — to recognize that the chaos has a name, a form of its own, a force: the name is sin, the evil of man that resists the love of God. When man praises this love, sin does not contradict him but simply goes underground and continues to belie in hidden ways his belief in God's love. This is why the revelatory mystery features, irreducibly, the *two* pairings: *God* the Father and *love*; *Christ* and *sin*. That love is true and not the projection of optimism, only because its obverse is a mystery of blood and expiation. The meeting between these two polarities, of Father-love and Christ-expiation, is the Holy Spirit.

At the deepest point of his adventure with God, man is brought to his own dark mystery, where God's love gets lost in his own tortuous self-hood, when God's love and his own flourishing refuse to coincide, and for a reason that he does not fully understand. At this point, however, God enables him to catch a glimpse of his true self, in which they do coincide: but this true self is separated from him in its beauty, and he finds himself its crucifier. With that world that resists the glory, he finds himself allied, as a crucifier. Here is the mystery of blood, and of God's love enfleshed as forgiveness.

If we proceed in this order, starting, that is, with man's psychic being, the point at which the Christ-Self begins to be history is just here – where the mystery of blood reveals itself. For the blood, says the psyche, is shed or it is nothing. It is now that the Christ becomes Jesus: on the cross. And from the Cross we as it were create history backward – down the life of Jesus back to his Virgin Birth.

Only the self, God's self, the self-for-God, is crucified, and only by the ego. The pattern is constant. The only variation is that I move from an extroverted position in regard to it, in which *I* am the crucifier, *he* the crucified, to a centred position where I acquire sufficient *selfhood* to be *identified* with the crucified. This is the transition from man who 'crucifies the Lord of Glory' to man who is 'nailed to the cross with Christ.' It is the same man, changing only through self-discovery in Christ.

3 MAKING PEACE BY THE BLOOD OF HIS CROSS

A further step has to be taken. I have said that God uses the crucifixion of Jesus to convince us that, even at our worst, as crucifiers of the good, we are accepted by him. But this way of putting the matter obscures the fact that there is a transcendental relationship between sin in its ultimate manifestation and the love of God. From the more homely point of view that we have been unfolding, God's forgiveness is greeted, as it occurs in the context of the crucifixion, with the cry 'even there!' But from a more radical point of view, we shall have to say 'especially there, essentially there, most clearly there, with finality there, finally there.' For evil brought to its essential self-expression necessarily encounters and succumbs to the love of God. Evil, that has always worked its way incognito into the whole life of the individual and society, once it gets inscribed, as it were, on the universe, encounters and is embraced within the love that is all-encompassing. 'Ah see, where Christ's blood streams in the firmament!' cries Marlow's Faustus. *That* is the sign of God's all-accepting love, *because* it is the at last adequate sign of evil. The blood that cries to heaven as the true emblem and symbol and meaning of sin, calls down the infinite love. We might pause to attempt some alternative wordings for this awesome idea.

In the ultimate order the ultimate sin, of crucifying the Just One, reverses itself, the victim giving life to the crucifiers. Sin, our deep, necessary, negative power, has no being. The only kind of 'being' it can have is the sight of itself in its ultimate effect, the crucified. This solution is uniquely God's. It is dimly glimpsed in an ultimate maturity of the spirit. For we have to experience God coming into us, taking our shape of sin, making explicit our sin, making sin work our salvation. The ultimate truth, which is God's unique embrace, is that the essential *effect* of sin – the crucified – is, identically, the heal-

8

ing. What sin ultimately *is*, is seen in the crucified. What sin ultimately *is*, is forgiven. For sin brought to its ultimate succumbs to God's love. It cannot be otherwise. If suffices for God to make our elusive evil explicit in crucifixion, for it to be no more. The crucified, therefore, *as* signifying sin's *ultimate* meaning, signifies its *forgiveness*. To *see* sin is to see its forgiveness. Man without the Christ cannot see sin, and so cannot see forgiveness.

This radical statement illuminates two great Pauline themes: that of the pervasive and elusive nature of sin until the final démarche when, in the crucifixion of Jesus, it at last finds expression and thus encounters the love of God, and that of the correspondence between Adam and Christ as consisting in the fact that in these two human situations alone sin is out in the open. The two themes combine. We have a picture of man, in his beginning, 'having it all together', knowing no split in himself between his creaturehood and his self-actualisation (Ernest Becker), or between spontaneity and will (Rahner on 'concupiscence'), or between nature and civilization (George B. Leonard and S. Moore), man in such a position, that is, that the admission of evil will have the clear form of rebellion against God. The first sin committed in this condition is the last that will have this clarity until the New Man makes possible the resumption of this ultimate dialogue of man with his God. To describe the nature of sin during this interim is to describe a complex history of disguises, partial disclosures, and correspondingly partial remedies.

This history is one of the themes of Romans. Rahner sums it up thus:

' . . . the Sin which appears in the world and affects all men in consequence of Adam's act is not regarded by St. Paul as a purely static deprivation of the spirit suffered by Adamite man; rather this primal and hereditary sin contains a dynamic and active element which urgently seeks to reveal its own nature in the personal sins of the individual. Thus *the* Sin comes into the world like a ruler (Rom 5:12), 'dwells' in man's flesh (Rom 7:20), subjects man to itself as its slave (Rom 6:6.17.20; 7:14), revives through the experience of the Law (Rom 7:8.9), in this way becomes manifest in man's concrete life (Rom 7:13) by subjecting man to its law (Rom 7:23); 8:2) and using his 'members' as its weapons (Rom 6:13). (Theological Investigations Vol 1 347 n.2)

The situating of history as interim between the two clear 'men', and the consequent theological symmetry between the two 'men', is clearly stated by Paul. The period that best exemplifies the *confusion* that follows the original loss is the period from Adam to Moses. 'But death held sway from Adam to Moses, even *over those who had not sinned as Adam did, by disobeying a direct command* – and *Adam foreshadows the Man who was to come.*' (Rom 5.14)

During the period of the Law, evil could once again assume its proper form of 'disobeying a direct command', but *this* disobedience was a mere shadow of the clear Adamic disobedience. For this is a situation in which man, faced with the alternatives of obedience and disobedience, does not know himself and answers to the classic description in Romans 7.14ff. 'We knew that the law is spiritual, whereas I am weak flesh sold into the slavery of sin. I cannot even understand my own actions. I do not do what I want to do but what I hate. When I act against my own will, by that very fact I agree that the Law is good. This indicates that it is not I who do it but sin which resides in me.' Sin maintains its diffused and not fully enfleshed condition in us. It has us doing evil, but not through the unambiguous decision of our total being. And just as the disobedience of man under the Law fails to reproduce the disobedience of Adam, so his obedience under the Law fails to be that obedience from which Adam defected. And thus, while what cancels the disobedience of Adam is a new obedience, this is nothing less than the reappearance of the total man amidst the human chaos. In this new context, the obedient man has to be crucified by the evil that, incognito, pervades the human. Evil, unmasked as the crucifier of the true man, knows itself for the first time and, for the first time, confronts that which alone prevails over and must prevail over evil, namely God's love.

But the more we succeed in clarifying this Pauline logic, the more we are driven to seek out the *interiority* of the process which it describes. What is it in man that God seeks, whose flourishing is God's glory, whose neglect seems unavoidable in the self-building of man, and whose crucifixion might lay bare what the whole conspiracy of history has hidden, and open the way to a new outpouring of the Spirit of God in human hearts and in human community? What is this centre to which Jesus gives expression and calls into existence in a dark mystery of expiation? Who *are* we, that we are *thus* lost, *thus* rediscover ourselves, and are *thus* recovered by an all-encompassing love?

10

To answer this question is a delicate matter. Yet it is hardly to be doubted that the answer has to be on the lines of a distinction between the ego and the self. Generically – and with all the weakness inherent in a generic statement – evil consists in an infinite variety of alienation between the conscious ego of man and a total self in which he has his place in God's world. And so generically, salvation consists in the overcoming of this protean alienation. But even apart from the question of its Christological understanding, this generic statement is hedged, for the wise practitioner of Jungian theory, by an almost despairing caution: he who comes to some sense of what is called the self comes under an almost insuperable temptation to claim this realization 'for himself', to appropriate it in terms of the ego. Such a person becomes the mystagogue for whom the mystery of human totality has become a pretension and has *replaced* the need to live out the life of the ego in its context of history and society. For the wise, on the contrary, the coming into the self is expressed only in silent contemplation, in humility, and in the indefinable benefits which the wise confer on the less aware.

Now this caution, this restricted but most precious application of the paradigm of ego and self, is most eloquently exemplified in our approach to the mystery of Jesus Christ. For to come into that mystery, I must give more serious weight than in the Jungian praxis to the fact that I am in large part outside it. The articulation of *this* factor for the Christian, *his* way of recognizing the ego in its whole political complex, *his* way of not short-circuiting salvation, is to say: I recognize myself, in the total context of this mystery, as the sinner brought to consciousness and sorrow as the crucifier of the self, that is not 'my best self' or 'my full potential', or any other of our pretentious euphemisms, but is symbolized most truly by a sinless man crucified on a hill, for whose crucifixion I gladly accept liability within a mystery of God's all-encompassing love. As I accept *that* position, in meditation and in the praxis of life, I may be led, in the spiritual logic of the mystery and under the sway of the Spirit, to a growing inward sense of *that which is crucified*. But as long as I live in this world, my life will move – in rhythm with all the complexities of being a participant in the mystery of evil and its redemption – between the poles of crucifier and crucified. In short, the self-experience of the believer as crucifier and crucified is the most acute and committed form of that self-experience between the poles of ego

11

and self that is the fruit of a Jungian self-understanding.

The following lines from Eliot's play 'The Family Reunion' provide a poetic summary of the history of sin:

> It is possible that sin may strain and struggle
> In its dark instinctive birth, to come to consciousness
> And *so* find expurgation. (emphasis mine)

4 THE LAMB SLAIN FROM THE FOUNDATION OF THE WORLD

Man has a secret, operative in all that he desires, wills, and creates. It is, that, finally, he does not believe in himself. Balancing all his achievements, there is the death-wish. The latter reaches, in times of crisis and decay like the present, a dangerous degree of overtness. But even in the time of flowering, it was there. Not only does man know that he will die. He lets this fact speak to him of the vanity of all that he strives for.

But this will-not-to-be is no mere weakness. It *resists* the power which calls man into being and which, in his consciousness, calls him to being, to identity, to personhood, to himself. The will-not-to-be desires to undo the order of being that represents this power, to make it not the case that man is called to an ever-greater intensity of selfhood.

This is the mystery of evil, of which we have many occasions to be conscious. Evil is the inability of the death-wish to be simply a death-wish: its necessity to justify itself by removing the very *grounds* for requiring of us a more intensely personal life. This shows itself in the resentment that is sometimes felt in the presence of an exceptionally good and courageous man. The desire to remove him is the desire to remove an unusually eloquent piece of evidence for the fact that we are called to full personhood. The most passionately protected thing in us is our mediocrity, our fundamental indecision in respect of life. Its protection will require, and will not stop at, murder.

It might be thought that once this conspiracy of cowardice in face of being is exposed to us, we would be able to overcome it. But this is not so. This inertial force of evil in us has the power of a fear that we do not understand, a fear that would be overcome only by some extraordinary new birth of love in us, in response to some new revelation.

Christianity offers itself as this revelation, this goad to love. Its way of dissolving the inertia of evil is so simple yet so extraordinary that we feel impelled to say that it *is* in the nature of revelation. For the resolution consists in provoking us to act out, in a uniquely total way, our desire for the good and the true and the wholly personal not to be there. It presents us with the vision of Jesus, the man without evil in him, destroyed simply because he *is* without evil. It invites us, under the pressure of a new force called Holy Spirit, to discover ourselves in that classic murder, and to experience, in this avowed aversion to the good, acceptance of us by the power that makes all things. More essentially, it invites us to experience our evil as never before, at last unmasked, to experience our decent death-wish as murder, and *in* that experience to feel for the first time the love that overpowers evil.

Thus, at the threshold of our advance into full personhood, there takes place not simply a new incentive but a crisis, in which the dark power of evil in us finds at last its appropriate and beautiful object and destroys it. And what then? The 'what then?' situation does not otherwise arise. When it does arise, there is and can be only love. Love is that which can only reveal itself to us in the total expenditure of our hatred of being. Only love can be there: and love can only be there.

In this crisis, our identity, that we have shied away from, floods into us on a tide of love. It is only by a total surrender that we come into our identity, a surrender whose dimensions embrace the deep mystery of our refusal and has required, for its being made, the full experience of that refusal. Another way of putting this is to say that the beauty into which being-fearful man comes is crucified. The image of the crucified is the glory of man as we know him, of that man that we are.

He who enters ever more deeply into the vision of the crucified, in which evil becomes sin and sin becomes forgiveness, finds, in an ultimate mystery, his own identity. He knows at last who he is. He knows at last the being that he has dreaded and desired to be. He experiences this identity as liberation from 'the world', from the whole customary complex web of conspiracy that is its systematic denial. He cannot praise sufficiently the blood that that world has shed.

And he clings to the figure on the cross not with the desperation of man in search of a saviour but with the passion with which we embrace the being that God calls us to.

The specific beauty of the crucified is the beauty of man's identity. In contrast the whole life of historical man appears as typed: a human stereotype as opposed to the real being. In the man on the cross I find an identity and a world to live it in, that my education and my gradual acceptance of it declared to be impossible. No poet has conveyed more vividly than Wordsworth the contrast between human promise and human fact, but Wordsworth's contrasted splendour is the innocence of childhood:

> Heaven lies about us in our infancy:
> Shades of the prison-house begin to close
> Upon the growing Boy

whereas the true splendour is a transfiguration of evil with love.

In this vision, man of the city becomes man of the universe. The former's affair is with the institutions of his own creating. Only through the crucifixion of Jesus does man act out this ritualised denial of ultimate identity to the point where it becomes an affair with the universe beyond the city. For only faced with the good that he has destroyed because it is good, does man say, not to the city but to the stars, 'this is what I am'.

The mystic seeks an ultimate identity. He is impelled forward by the inadequacy of all the city's answers to his self-questioning. He may well see in the Christ-figure the powerful symbol of the self that he seeks to become. If he is realistic, his Christ-figure will be crucified. But the only way in to this identity with the figure on the cross is *via* the sinfulness that has put him there. *This* dimension, of the confessed crucifier, is the vigour, the honest humanity, the political realism, of his commitment to an ultimate human identity and mission.

No hero-figure can sustain the contemplation of being-hungry man, save the crucified. The Letter to the Hebrews says 'without the shedding of blood there is no remission.' We have become accustomed to stop at the *exegesis* of that text, relating it only to a primitive world of religious discourse. But it is not that without blood God is not satisfied. It is that without blood our root evil is still in hiding, so that we are not yet prepared or able to hear God. In this context, one of the new Mass canons has 'see the Victim whose death has reconciled *us* to yourself.' We need the blood, not God.

The bloodstained figure flashes back to us as betrayal what we otherwise experience as the ordinary and accepted limit on our potential. This is the foundational instance of consciousness-raising. In the crucified, man sees the cost of identity, and the betrayal of it, and, in the love that he feels coming into him, the transformation of the betrayal into the paying of the price. This new exercise of the heart's affections changes the world on which a man looks out. He will forever return to question the crucified who has given to his immemorial involvement with ultimate reality the embarrassing, bewildering, and gloriously obvious character of sexual intimacy.

Finally, it is impossible to live with this mystery of the crucified as the symbol that transforms evil into sin and sin into forgiveness, without coming to see that this crucified embrace of God *anticipates* all evil, and the conscious creation that must carry the potential for evil, as well as *embracing* evil after it has become fact. The scholastic distinction between an 'antecedent' will of God, that does not contain the cross, and a 'consequent' will of God that does, misses the enormity of what the cross reveals of God. Christ's blood streams in the firmament of the beginning, as the sign of the universe it is to be, one, that is, whose hidden pitfalls themselves open onto the new fulness of being. The cross of Jesus, as sign of the power of love over evil, is appropriately placed at any point in space-time. It is trivial to regard the creation of potentially sinful man as 'a risk that God took', with the cross of Jesus as the remedy God applied when the risk became disaster. Such an account fails to see the difference between saying that God is able to draw good out of evil and the more radical statement that God's love *embraces* evil. This is not to say that there is evil in God. It is to say that God is a reality in which evil is mysteriously transmuted. Not the philosopher's evil that is pure negation and easily seen to cancel out in God, but that evil which, short of God, is the most real thing with which man has to deal, and whose succumbing to God in his heart will cost him and give him everything. And *this* radical statement about God and evil comes close to saying something about *God*, about his *character*. It suggests that God is prepared to *push* man into evil and beyond into the vision of the heart of being. Evil is not so much an obstacle that

God can overcome, as a tool in his hands. As the symbol of *this* sort of God, a God we cannot get at *short* of evil and who therefore in some way wants us through evil (in the sense of wanting my son through law-school!) the cross of Jesus is appropriately placed as the foundation of the created universe. And Revelation speaks of 'the Lamb that was slain from the foundation of the world' (13,8).

5 THE RECOGNITION OF JESUS

Jesus Christ, in the experience of the believer, is a man who lived two thousand years ago. But he is this man *recognized* as the expression, as the personality, of something in the soul or psyche of the believer as a human being.

What is this 'something'? It is the person's life, sensed – however obscurely – as hungry for some ultimate meaningfulness, convinced of some ultimate meaningfulness. It is the root of rare moments of an unaccountable happiness. It is what all idealists and reformers draw upon. It is why there *are* idealists and reformers. It is a spark of the divine. It is what Augustine is talking about when he says 'Thou has made us for thyself, and our heart is restless till it rests in thee.' 'Our heart', in that statement, is 'this something'. God's destining us 'for himself' is, however obscurely, *experienced* as restlessness, and, even more obscurely, as promise. There is promise in us. And this 'promise' is a promise of life. It has to do, not with something we want to get, but with being ourselves without any inhibition. The greatest happiness possible, and the very definition of happiness, is to be oneself without any inhibition. And Augustine is saying that we can only be this way 'in God'.

The recognition of Jesus as 'this' is the work of the Holy Spirit in a person. The Spirit alone has the subtlety and closeness to the individual's life to awake, in response to the image of Jesus, his very own sense of desirable being, what *he* would give everything for. It is the Spirit that roots Jesus in the ongoing history of the individual. And while what the individual experiences, and 'would give anything for', is simply 'Jesus', the motif for this experience and love is being woven out of the most essential substance of the lover's soul. The saints whose profession of love for Jesus takes extravagant and sometimes embarrassing forms, are people who have allowed the

Spirit to make conscious, to a degree far in excess of the normal, this inner core of humanity in them, and to identify it with Jesus. In other words the love for Jesus has, under the Spirit, a very strong subjective component: nor is it possible without this. And thus Paul can say 'no one can say "Jesus is Lord" except in the Holy Spirit'. It is not simply that the Spirit tells the believer that Jesus is Lord. The Spirit tells *this* believer what 'Lord' means in his or her life.

But to say that this psychic marriage between Jesus and the believer's innermost reality is the work of the Spirit is not to deny to that marriage all other intelligibility. Something of the subjective component, of the human ideal, is spelt out in the traditional formulations of faith. Thus for a people whose thirst for the fuller life crystallized in the figure of an eschatological Messiah-King, 'Jesus the Christ' means, 'Jesus the embodiment of our desire'. Now the name 'Jesus Christ' as it is repeated countless times every day in the liturgies of the Christian world, *is no longer doing that job* – and that job has to be done. Similarly, the really important thing about calling Jesus the Logos is the intense human passion that once crystallized in that expression. These titles, which originally linked the Jesus of history to the human psyche in its generation of human meanings, lost this force and became abstract theological titles locating him in a system of belief rather than in the psyche and experience of man. As a result, people lost the capacity to see Jesus as the reflection of *their own* deepest lives, feelings, aspirations.

Not only do those ancient titles no longer fire the soul of the believer, but we are now into the era of 'psychological man': man is beginning to be in touch with that psychic centre whence, in an earlier time, he naively projected his image of the consummated or ideal man – the Christ image for instance. This centre Jung calls 'the self'. He means the obscurely perceived totality of a person's life as a reality able to become conscious and to be a source of psychic energy far in excess of and more far-reaching than the self of which we are readily and inescapably conscious and which we call ego. My life is so much more than me.

A new title for Jesus is beginning to form in people's lives. He is 'the self'. This title is basic to the way of understanding Jesus and his saving Passion that is worked out in this book.

This understanding of Jesus as 'the self' is, in the primary sense, deeply traditional. It is carrying on the traditional and indispensable practice of relating Jesus to man's self-understanding. It is, in the terms set by 'psychological man', making overt the subjective component in people's faith in Jesus. More precisely, it is doing what must be done for this subjective component in the area of a shared and explicated belief. It remains true, of course, that only the Holy Spirit *makes* Jesus the transforming symbol of my innermost life, of the inward shape of my motivation. But to cooperate in this making I need self-knowledge – as the Christian mystical tradition has consistently maintained. I need to be pointed, and by the confident instruction of a shared faith, to that spacious country of myself that lies in the shadow of the ego, in order to experience its coming together in Jesus. I need also a vivid sense of my impatient and fearful ego-life as riding roughshod over that fine country, crucifying my 'Lord of glory'. And I need to experience this situation as, in recollection, the forgiveness situation, whence spring the energies of the new man.

To this end, I am developing this practice: when I hear in the liturgy a text like this: 'He has made known to us his hidden purpose – to be put into effect when the time was ripe: namely, that the universe, all in heaven and on earth, might be brought into a unity in Christ' (Eph 1, 9–10), I look inward. I think, when I hear the name 'Christ', of the vast inner resources of personhood and freedom and sacrifice that God is awakening in me as I fix before my eyes Jesus crucified. In other words, I consciously shift the centre of gravity of the Pauline gratitude to God for Christ. That centre has been 'Christ, out there'. Paradoxically, the more the Christian psyche has been disabled through a weakening of the Christian subjective component, the more it has fastened on the 'Christ out there'. To anyone conversant with psychology this is not a paradox. The less we get from people and things outside us (owing to a failure within), the more we seek our weal just there. The mother-deprived person keeps going to the mother and her surrogates for life.

In John's gospel Jesus says 'he who believes in me, out of his interior will come a fountain of living water, springing up to eternal life'. That is what it is to believe in Jesus. It is to have one's own flood-gates opened. Into the image of Jesus on the cross, wood and nails and all, the psyche pours its endless and otherwise forgotten life.

6 THE STRUCTURE OF SELF-DISCOVERY THROUGH THE IMAGE OF JESUS

I most deeply and accurately discover Jesus as the man I never was, only when I realise that my not being wholly a man is what crucifies him. Jesus on the cross represents an identity which I am crucifying rather than entering. But my crucifying is my way of entry, for it represents my non-personhood forced into its characteristic action, which is the destruction of wholeness. So there I am, out in the open at last. But once out in the open, I lose the fight to keep what I *thought* was myself but was really my anonymity. Forced to hear myself saying 'I hate that which makes for life', I expose myself to sorrow, and sorrow, if I give it free rein, bears me in to the heart of the crucified where I discover myself. Thus I am reborn in the identity that I have sought to fend off by crucifying. The way into this identity is the way of the spear: that is precisely why the crucified is the symbol of our lost and recovered identity. We crucify Jesus rather than be him, and thus, through the healing power of sorrow, we become him.

As I enter further and further into this mystery of blood and new birth, I see the sins of my past ever more clearly as expressions of *fear*. Fear was the point. Fear of that centre where there is no fear. And as the centre, discovered, shows up fear as hate, the fear thus exposed revives in memory as the heart of sin and the key to so much past behaviour.

Only Christianity has the effrontery to *answer* the question 'what are we afraid of?' For Christianity, it is the least rhetorical of questions. At its centre is the symbol that transmutes fear into hate and hate into sorrow and forgiveness. Or, in more generic terms, evil into sin and sin into sorrow and forgiveness.

If it is conceded that symbolism is the most powerful form of communication, and that a philosophy of man requires to find symbolic form if it is to touch man to the heart and move him, can it be doubted that the symbolism of the crucified is the most potent expression and resolution of the tragic drama of man's wrestle with himself?

7 A NOTE ON THE CULT OF SUFFERING

One of the things that earns Christianity a bad name is the cult of suffering.

And how does Christianity clear itself of the charge, with its talk of desiring to be nailed to the cross with Christ?

It cannot, so long as it ignores the unique saving power of *Jesus'* suffering and the *way* we come to identify with the man on the cross. To understand the suffering of Jesus as the effect of my evil is to understand it as the suffering I am inflicting on my true self. Conversion, which operates through sorrow, consists in shifting my position from the crucifying ego to the crucified self. Jesus makes first conscious and then salvific the suffering that is inherent in our evil, alienated condition.

But if the suffering of Jesus is not seen as a place of self-discovery, if it is not seen as saving and the saving as self-discovery, then we find ourselves simply 'identifying with a sufferer', choosing *him* as our hero because of some belief in the value of suffering.

Jesus, whose life reveals its meaning on the cross, is not for imitation. The agony in which his earthly life ends, while it is chosen by him and freely willed, is not chosen by him as a way of life but embraced by him as the necessary correlative of his sinlessness in a sin-world. *This* choice, which must be mysterious to us, is not like the choice to pursue virtue or wisdom – that is to say, not like the choices that we admire and try to imitate in our heroes. It would be a disastrous mistake to class Jesus' choice of suffering with Solomon's choice of wisdom. It would make a masochist of him and of his followers.

We do not follow in the footsteps of a sufferer: we find ourselves in the suffering that, understood as our infliction, resolves the evil in our condition. The reason why Jesus is not for imitation is not that he is beyond our scope or understanding, but that he is the identity of each of us.

Jesus on the cross frees man from that which puts him there. Who is 'him'? Well, Jesus: but also that which Jesus represents, which is the wholeness of man.

We need a new concept of this wholeness. We have considered man, and the evil in him which sets him against the order in which he is called to truth and goodness and personhood. But this is not simply an order *in* which man is called wholly to be: it is the man he is called to be: it is man's wholeness already known as his, as himself, beckoning to him, feared and crucified by him. It cannot be too much insisted that man's evil is turned, in the deepest analysis, on himself. In it he hates *himself* as the free being he knows himself to be. He hates himself free. Which means, he hates himself free from evil. He hates himself free from sin. So, he hates himself as he sees himself in Jesus, the man free from sin. What Jesus shows is that there where man should above all love himself, he hates himself. And this hate, *directly* opposed to his wholeness as it only is in the drama of Jesus, succumbs to it in a new birth of the whole man in blood.

Thus Jesus does not take man off the cross: but he frees him from putting himself there. And ever after there appears in human life a distinction between suffering self-imposed through fear, and suffering not thus self-imposed. The latter is the lot of the victims of the power-hungry and manipulative. The former is the lot of the power-hungry and manipulative.

One of the most important lessons we learn from the cross is that the wicked, the destroyers of lives and of life, are sufferers. The appeal Jesus on the cross makes to them is to see *themselves* as the victim of their malice.

The deepest and strongest peace a man can have is when he stops running away – when, that is, he *need* no longer run away, for it is a poor and nervous peace that one gains by merely forcing oneself to stop this flight. Peace is the cessation of man's flight from himself in the power of a new revelation.

What can *stop* this flight by rendering it unnecessary? The resolution of the fear that impels it. And what a fantastic resolution of this fear takes place when, forced to turn into hate and crucify, it then succumbs to love! At ever greater depths of himself, a man will see the bloodstained figure that contains the greatest peace that man can ever know: the peace that is the end of the otherwise endless logic of destruction that is the way of evil.

We seem to have touched here another theme, non-violence. A theology of non-violence sees the redemptive action of Christ as consisting in a final, total because non-retaliative, acceptance of violence. But this is not a separate theme. For the fact that violence provokes retaliatory violence is only a special case of the general theorem that violence, until the total resolution, has to go on. Man in flight from himself is intrinsically violent, and this violence *not only* provokes further violence but *itself* proceeds to ever fresh violence. The resolution in the crucified is more radical than that which consists in non-retaliation. For it is the cessation of *that which provokes* retaliatory violence. Thus a theology of non-violence cannot afford the *principle* for a theology of redemption. It is itself derivative from the transformation of evil into sin and sin into love, which is the transforming symbolism of the crucified.

Man's self-hatred is not adequately expressed in the *interactive* process of violence provoking violence. It resides in the heart of man that is the seat of evil. The heart of man is not converted simply by seeing that the other to whom his violence is directed does not return it. The heart of man is converted by seeing that his violence is directed to himself: to himself dramatized in the symbol of Jesus crucified where he (man) appears as most lovable and most hated, and, in sorrow and pardon, most whole.

In sum, what the crucified Jesus is forever bringing to an end is not simply the otherwise endless process of violence provoking violence, but what itself powers this process, the endless fear of man for himself, the endless flight of man from himself, the endless crucifixion of man by himself. That which stops at the crucified and so enters into peace is more than can ever be seen working itself out between men: it is the unfreedom, in a man's past and present, that is uncovered and cleared at ever greater depths of contemplation of Jesus making peace by the blood of his cross.

To invoke a powerful image from Ayn Rand, the symbol of Jesus crucified is addressed not simply to man the violent but to that deeper desperation that is driven to kill 'in order not to let himself know that the death he desires is his own'.

But it will be urged that the practice of non-retaliation does precisely what I am claiming that the Jesus-symbol does: tells the destroyer that it is himself he is destroying.

It is true that the non-violent response to violence throws the violent person back into himself. As long as the response is violent, the violent person feels justified, can go on believing that his hate has an object other than himself. The other person is unwittingly cooperating in my game of saying that it's not me that I hate, not me that I fear, not me that I'm unhappy with. This applies also to the whole theorem of transference and counter-transference. By 'transference' I put my guilt, my self-hatred, into you. Once you pick this up and start reacting, once, that is, you unwittingly let my transference become in you a 'counter-transference', you are backing me up in my flight-from-self. This means that reality, your reality, some reality other than myself, is backing me up in my flight-from-self. (The making of you guilty and wretched *is* my flight-from-self in action. It is not merely the *consequence* of my flight. It *is* it. *You* are where I am running to from myself.) And when you spot what is happening, and stop the counter-transference, you cut off the corroboration you have been affording me. I am thrown back on myself, and forced to carry on *in there* the business that I have been much more satisfactorily and satisfyingly carrying on *with you*. I founder. There is a horrendous description of this event in an extreme form at the end of 'Atlas Shrugged', when the supreme phoney, who has been applying electrical torture to the good man, suddenly realises in this the whole of his life and past as a grotesque act of self-loathing.

But here there is no healing. The tortured man becomes for the torturer 'a pretext that has totally broken down as a pretext', 'an alibi that has driven out the wretch who sought shelter in it', 'a moratorium on the inward hell that has expired, driving the torturer back into the inward hell'. In our affair with the crucified, on the other hand, the tortured man becomes a *symbol* of the self, the beauty, of the torturer. The beautiful tortured body of Ayn Rand's hero says in effect to the torturer 'take your dirty problem away from me, where it has no place, and bury it with yourself in the hell where you belong'. The tortured body of Jesus says to the torturer 'I am yourself, your beauty, which you are crucifying.' That is the specific nature and power of a symbol: the power of the other, of the not-me, to represent my wholeness to me. That is the essence of the believer's vision of Jesus crucified: that the tortured man shows to me my crucified wholeness in a way that is full of invitation and hope, a way that invites me, as into my home, into the self that I am crucifying.

I would like to clarify this difference between these two torture-situations. The Ayn Rand one illustrates the power of the facts to destroy the cheat, once that power has surfaced. In the confrontation of man with Jesus crucified, this same power of fact operates invitingly not repellingly. And this *gathering* as opposed to *disintegrating* force of truth is what we call its symbolic communication. We might *define* symbolic communication as the communication of awful truth invitingly. But this is not a sugaring of the pill. The point is that the true symbol, the Jesus symbol, makes the unbearable truth of ourselves bearable through the power of love. It makes the centre bearable not by disguising it but by attracting us into it. It puts the truth there for life not for death.

By the *facts* I am found out. By the *symbol* I am found. Interesting, that expression 'found out'. It implies that when the inspector called I was out! I was not on the spot. I was off-centre. I was not in control. And all these images refer to that falling-short of personhood that is the essence of evil.

The *manner* of this invitation, of this attractive and leading way of saying 'I am you though you will not see it', is, as I have said, symbolic. But this word 'symbolic' here only names the structure, the manner, the style, of the communication. Something immense is required to *make* and *empower* this symbol of the crucified in the citadel of the soul. That 'something' is the historically reported goodness of Jesus, combined with the psyche's deepest power to project in symbol its drama of self-crucifixion, these two components fused in the power of the Holy Spirit, the spirit of wholeness.

There is another way of expressing this distinction between non-violent response by itself and the full meaning of the crucified. To be changed I need *not only* to be chased out of hating myself *in* another, *but also* brought to seeing the self, that I hate, *as* other, as a man

27

abandoned on a cross. I need to say '*there* is my life, my beauty, my possibility, my humanness, my full experience as a human which is a personifying of the universe, my outrageously ignored and neglected dream of goodness'. And *that* welcomes me. That *means* me. That is my meaning. That is my symbol. That is my sacrament. That is my baptism. That is my bread and wine. That is my love. The self that we hide in others in order to neglect and destroy it there, needs to be seen symbolically, whole-makingly, *as* another, before we can appropriate it. Its otherness is the spur to sorrow, which is the organ of its appropriation.

I am talking about the difference between two sorts of symbol. There is the personal symbolism whereby I invest other people with my hopes, my ambitions, and my guilt. And there is the great transpersonal symbol of the crucified whole, that draws for its power not on the desperate and diverse politics of our self-evasion but on the deepest resources of the psyche where it is touched by that power that creates and holds and promotes all being. The breaking-down of our personally constructed symbols, in the undoing of our transferences, is indispensable to our growth as persons. But it is a fatal error to go to this demytheologisation for the model of the saviour-encounter.

9 IS THERE ANY SORROW LIKE UNTO MY SORROW?

The mystery of the cross makes explicit the suffering that is implicit in the reign of sin. Just as it makes explicit, as sin – as the clear Adamic sin redivivus – the evil that pervades human life: just as it dramatizes as an act of wilful *destruction* of the whole man our habitual practical *negation* of the whole man, so this mystery features, in a fully explicit form, the *suffering* that this destruction inflicts.

This raises an extraordinarily delicate question. We have seen that it is only in the context of a person's encounter with the crucified in faith that this prodigious making-explicit of evil as sin takes place. Neither the members of the Sanhedrin, nor Pilate, nor the soldiers, performed *this* critical all-evil-expressing sin of man. Only a person who, faced with the crucified, is awakening to all his depths, sees in those depths, as the crucifying of the Christ, the evil that has pervaded all his life. But the question is: if none of the *agents* in the drama performed this sin, did the man on the cross *suffer* it?

I have to give an affirmative answer here. There is in the encounter with the crucified, in which certainly the archetypal potential of the psyche is stretched to the full, a mystery of concreteness, I would almost dare to say a smell of blood. Although it is myself that is coming alive in the encounter: although it is a self far wider and deeper than that of common experience that is coming into individuality as my own: nevertheless there is, as an essential part of the encounter, a man, not myself, who suffers much.

There is something strange here. It might appear that 'communion with an archetypal suffering Christ' and 'historical recalling of a man who once suffered' are two perfectly distinct operations, neither one requiring the other. But these alternatives so understood do not fit the Christian contemplative experience. It is as though my recognition of myself in the suffering Christ, which is necessarily and consciously incomplete and progressive in nature, demands, as the corrollary of this incompleteness and the support for this progress, that the portion of the Christ that I have *not* yet appropriated be concretely realised in someone, and not merely reside in the inexhaustible archetype. At every stage of my personal entry into the mystery, the Christ that I have *not* yet become is a man who somehow *is*, and not a platonic anthropos-image. This tension seems to be essential to the encounter. Resolve it by dissolving the thought of the Jesus who actually was on that cross, and the encounter itself, with all its power to evoke in me the self, falls to pieces.

We can enlarge this picture. We have seen that the believer relates to Christ as part crucifier and part crucified, there being between these two an infinite number of gradations. In so far as I am not finding myself in the crucified, I am the penitent crucifier, and so I shall be, and so every believer will be, until death. And in so far as I am the crucifier, the crucified is other, is not-I. And the only meaningful representation of this not-I is a real person, another human being. Make of *him* simply the as yet unappropriated self, and the tension and realism of the encounter collapses. The suffering-of-sin that I have not yet found in myself and found myself in, is in a real body nailed to a cross.

Or we might put it this way. While it is my true self that I progressively *discover* in the contemplation of the crucified, it is not 'my true self' that I there *explore*. The field of exploration, that which underspans the exploration, is the man on the cross. And while it is perhaps impossible to say exactly what this means, the suffering in which man in his evil situation becomes critically explicit had to become explicit *first* in a man. That man must appear to me as one step ahead of me in the growth in identity that is mine in the encounter. And the identity in which he is ahead of me is not located merely in the indefinite potentiality of the archetype. It is nailed to a cross.

Supposing we took the Bultmannian approach, conceding that there had to be *someone* called Jesus upon whom the whole thing could be built up: that someone could be any pious man who suffered what is after all the fate of many pious men. Does that work? Absolutely not, for me. The consciousness of Christian myth as having *that* sort of historic foundation would not make the encounter with Jesus crucified significantly more concrete than if the whole affair were frankly said to be no more than the negotiation of an archetype.

Of course, once we have rejected the Bultmannian view, we create fresh problems. For are we not *then* committed to a historical Jesus who would consciously represent the Passion of all mankind? I think that we have absolutely no means, no terms, for the positive description of the type of consciousness that would be capable of that suffering which the Christian mind and heart learns to have been the suffering of Jesus.

It is in this context that we appreciate the economy and adequacy – we might say the elegance – of the New Testament clue: the man without sin. This is potent double negative: and a double negative communicates in a very peculiar way. What is 'a man without sin' like? We don't know, in the ordinary way. I think that this phrase speaks best to – and is meant to speak to – the faithful encounter with the crucified. It describes, not genius or any known human excellence (except goodness, which ultimately *is* an elusive quality anyhow), but only *that* individual human reality that the Christian soul intuits, in the manner I have suggested, as underlying and forever standing ahead of the encounter.

10   THE MEANING OF SIN

As the main contention of this book is that the forgiveness of sin is the central idea of the New Testament, it is necessary to clarify the meaning of sin. There is an ambiguity in the concept of sin that creates untold confusion.

The two senses in the word 'sin' are: a defect that is predicated *of* the human condition; and a defect observed *within* the human condition, by some people in others, by some people in themselves, taking an enormous number of forms. The first sense has for its point of reference some order embracing the whole of reality and equated by the believer with the mind of God: in relation to this order it makes sense to say that 'man' fails, resists, refuses. The second sense has for its point of reference the *human* order as expressed in this or that culture, with the possibility that we may find a few offenses recognised as such by all cultures: in this order all offenses are judged in relation to the world of meanings constituted by man.

More simply, the first sense of sin relates it to a world of which man is *not* the centre, while the second relates it to a world of which man *is* the centre.

The use of the one word in both these senses is as embarrassing as it would be if we had one word which sometimes meant 'colour', at other times meant 'red'.

Clearing up this ambiguity would seem to be a simple matter. For who will not be struck by the difference between man's 'failure of the Universe' and an action like theft or murder or rape? And yet it is not so simple. For there is an overlap between the two meanings of sin. It would be morally insensitive to say that rape is ultimately sinful only in the sense that cathedrals are ultimately sinful: that is to say, to *reserve* the ultimate meaning of sin for man's sense of himself as the centre of reality, a meaning no more or less verified in any one work of man than in any other. The human sense of self-centrality is

32

more clearly recognisable in some attitudes and actions than in others – that is to say, in those attitudes and actions that society recognises as bad. It being always understood that society has some huge blind spots, and that it is society that says to the individual 'allow me to remove the speck in your eye' while ignoring the plank in its own.

What we must concentrate on, then, is not the attitude or act that is being described as sinful, but the *horizon of meaning* against which it is being seen as sinful. And here the distinction is quite clear. On the one horizon of meaning, rape is the action of a man choosing his own gratification in despite of the dignity of another, of himself, and of the whole social order. On the other horizon, it is the action of a man choosing himself as he immediately experiences himself, against all possible and conceivable reality, against God.

But even here, a difficulty has to be noticed. To confine ourselves to the 'ultimate horizon' would be, for most of us, to weaken our moral sense. Imagine the fulminations of the prophets against extortion, oppression of the poor, and pride, deprived of the natural moral indignation of man as he contemplates the inequities within the human world. Nevertheless, this very fact that the thought of God is not enough for us as moral sensitizer shows that 'the thought of God' is incredibly weak in us, corresponding hardly at all to the flaming and all-consuming reality. And this indeed is sin, in a meaning now very close to the one it is to have when we consider the forgiveness of sin in Christ. The whole theme of the gospel is that the 'ultimate horizon' is becoming near, vivid, and, for those who become open to it, all-controlling. This is the Reign of God. And in this perspective we can see what sin is. Sin is the unreality of God. Sin is the unreality of the real to the unreal. Sin is the unreality of life other than the small portion of it that one calls one's own and builds into immobility. Sin is a monumental indifference to the totality of which one is a part and is otherwise without meaning. Once this is understood, certain things become clear. First, the forgiveness of sin, the unhardening of the heart, is the most urgently desirable grace, and will be central to any religion that takes both God and man seriously. Secondly, the more monstrous human evils such as the Nazi camps, easily seen by us to be evil, are cynically thorough applications of the sinful principle that is not so easily recognised. Thirdly, these obvious and repulsive manifestations of our evil exemplify the sin for which Jesus dies, only when they are so understood. Fourthly, the dramatic

33

difference between these great evils and the way we decent people live, easily leads us to go to them for our *concept* of sin, and thus to see sin as the *aberration* from a human norm rather than as the *exaggeration* of a human tendency. Fifthly, the idea of gross sin as aberration rather than exaggeration is ruinous to our understanding of the doctrine that Jesus died for our sins.

I have said that the ultimate horizon or perspective does not obliterate the distinctions observed in the shorter perspective, does not equate the rapist with the cathedral builder. But the *reason* why it does not do this is all-important: he who understands sin in the ultimate perspective has no concern with the comparison of action with action, whether to pronounce them unequal *or whether to equate them*. He is overcome with the enormity of human self-centredness in a universe of being whose centre is God.

He who awakens to this enormity in his own life will in all likelihood first do so in the context of those actions and attitudes that show up as sinful against the *nearer* horizon. The reason for this is that in such behaviour I can more clearly hear myself saying 'to hell with everything but me'. Thus the newly awakened Ignatius thought of his sexual promiscuity and daring. It takes considerable schooling in self-understanding to discover the 'to hell with everything but me' that underlies the most innocent attitudes and actions. This may be the reason why the gospel prefers prostitutes to pharisees. In a world where all are blind to the roots of behaviour, the gross sinner has a more colourful past in which he may see more clearly the choice of self against God. The pharisee has a spiritual subtlety that will stand him in good stead once the conversion process has got started, but that is liable to prevent its getting started at all.

The convert's recognition of his sinfulness in the context of 'near horizon' sins, also tends to contribute to the confusion between sin in its two horizons. The depravity of Ignatius and Augustine, so well-intended as an encouragement not to despair of the mercy of God, has the effect of disguising from us in what that mercy consists: the awakening of man from that deep sleep of which the grosser sins are but the nightmarish activation. Even the attitude of Jesus to prostitutes becomes counter-productive for theology. Presented as showing God's merciful approach to sinners, it conveys the assumption that 'prostitutes, for instance' are what 'sinners' *means*. And it isn't.

For none of the complexities in this question of sin, must be allowed to obscure or qualify the fact that when it is *redemption* from sin that we are considering, when it is that forgiveness that God gives in Christ, and especially when we say that the forgiveness of sin is the heart of the New Testament, we are referring exclusively to human behaviour seen against the 'ultimate horizon', where its enormity consists in the Godlike status that man implicitly claims for himself in all that he does and makes.

Conversely, where there is no realistic and convincing *notion* of this 'ultimate horizon' meaning of sin, of this sin *of man* as distinct from the sins of men, the mystery of the Redemption is bound to become a dead-letter. If what Christ saves us from is not some perceptibly awful fate, what is this salvation worth?

Here, however, we must make a distinction. Just as the Holy Spirit reveals Jesus to a person as his centre and true life, even when Christology is floundering, so the Holy Spirit instructs the faithful heart in the radical meaning of sin, even when the theology of salvation is confused. But when it is a question of getting this theology clear, we have to seek for a radical idea of sin not only in Spirit-directed meditation but in the area of a generally available human self-understanding.

Such self-understanding is becoming available. With the cumulative loosening of cultural assumptions it is becoming possible to see the whole human project from the outside as a necessary denial of an equally undeniable contingency, and so to see our whole history as characterised by this denial. The sin for which Christ died is no longer what, until this perspectival shift, it had to be, namely: a refusal of 'man' in respect of God, *symbolized* in the myth of Adam, and *somehow* present and operative in human history. That 'somehow', filled in by rhetorical descriptions of the human scene in which all human evils, from greed to death, were jumbled together, can now be replaced by a clear idea. Evil is operative in us as the denial of our contingency through fear, and as the cognate fascination with ourselves. It is the inescapable narcissism of consciousness. It is the denial of a contingency that finds its full acceptance only in Jesus on the cross where sin puts him and has to put him.

Thus the myth of Adam, out of which the Christian tradition of self-understanding has spun its yarn, becomes wedded to the myth of Narcissus, in which the psychoanalytic tradition of self-

35

understanding has seen the human trauma in its working-out. As the narcissistic interpretation of man breaks, with Becker, onto the ontological level, it pairs with the myth of Adam: the myth of Adam showing the price of *becoming* conscious, the Narcissus myth showing how that price is paid.

What is fascinating is, that the root of human evil as finally laid bare in a *secular* tradition of self-understanding yields a theory that is astonishingly similar to the Christian idea of sin. Let me try to explain this similarity. The denial of contingency explains at one and the same time the 'normal' and the 'abnormal' in human behaviour. For the 'normal' are those who achieve a relatively successful and socially accepted denial of contingency, while all the aberrations and perversions classified by psychoanalysis are so many bizarre and unlivable solutions. One basic formula – the denial of contingency – affords at once a better understanding of the 'abnormal' forms. And it does not merge the normal and the abnormal. On the contrary, a grasp of the root human evasion highlights how very *differently* different conditions of men do it. And this is not at all unlike the Christian idea of sin, which illuminates at one and the same time the consciousness of the decent person and the monstrous forms that sin can take. Note that I am not equating the monstrous sins with the psychological perversions. I am pointing to a significant similarity *of pattern. As* the perversions stand to normality in a world where *all* are denying the basic human truth, so the more glaring sins stand to the decent person in a world where all are denying to God his total reality. To the new psychological perspective, in which we are all, in a sense, mad, there corresponds the Christian perspective, in which we are all sinnners.

The new perspective, in which secular man sees himself as born into a life-problem that far exceeds the limits of ordinary self-awareness and is therefore a problem that is theological in all but *name*, is of the greatest significance for theology; theology which, on its side, has leaned too heavily on the *name* of the God who creates, questions, and draws us, rather than on the experience of being created, questioned, and drawn.

11 INTENSIFYING THE VISION

The meaning of the Christ-event is that in it the wrestle of man with his God-intended self is dramatized and led through the phases of rejection, hatred, crucifixion, destruction, surrender, new life. Oscar Wilde said 'Each man kills the thing he loves.' Those who stop short of evil in themselves will never know what love is about. They will never receive the crucified.

It is not for nothing, on the contrary it is in exact conformity with an exact law of the psyche, that the symbol in which evil is crystallised to the eternal renewal of life, could not be bettered as a symbol of man's futility. A body left to bleed to death on a cross. Death at its most eloquently indifferent to all that we try to believe in. All this is in order. In the all-sustaining power of God, evil has been allowed to express its triumph over man in a total symbol: a symbol whose totality is its undoing. The crucifixion of Jesus is the symbol in which evil tries to hold its own against God, and thus provokes the thunder of resurrection.

What I have, in the sight of Jesus on the cross, is not the *motive* for believing in God's love so that this belief will *then* overcome my self-hatred, but the actual *process*, made visible, dramatized in the flesh, whereby my self-hatred reaches its climax of realisation, avowal, confession, and surrender. Man's self-hatred is not only the *obstacle* to his acceptance of God's love. It is the *medium* in which God's love is revealed to him as it transforms it. I meet God's love not by turning away from the hatred of myself to another motif, but as a climax of my self-hatred, its crisis and resolution. God does not just give me a *reason* not to hate myself. He transforms my self-hatred into love. That is the meaning of the cross.

Once we realise that our sin *is* self-hatred, it becomes clear that Jesus, representing our self, suffers our sin. The suffering of Jesus is

37

the suffering that is the passive component in our sinful condition: it is that suffering, of the true self of man at the expense of the ego, that receives its full, symbolic, resolving expression in the crucifixion of Jesus where it receives the noble name of Passion.

In the mystery of Jesus, contemplated in faith, sinful man plunges, murderously, desperately, hopefully – who knows? – into the self with which he has ever been at odds: and there is accepted, there finds identity and freedom.

A powerful recentring of this mystery of love and blood is achieved once it is allowed that sin is in its essence self-hatred – the self-hatred that shows itself in man the more strong on him the touch of God becomes. But for *this* proposition to qualify for theological acceptance, the 'self' has to be the viceroy of God, a worthy *human* object of the sin that offends *him*. That is why the main probe of a reunified soteriology has to be an energetic and imaginative grappling with the sort of thing that Jung meant by 'the self'.

The standard account is less than incarnational. It secures the Incarnation *first*, as God's identity with Jesus, and *then* has Jesus on the cross expressing God's love. It does not dream of the awesome fact that God's love has become incarnate in a process that resolves the flesh's enmity with itself as his creation.

As we grow older, we become more sensitive to our interaction with other people. A huge fact begins to dawn on us: that no one is, or can be, neutral. Often it is the very people who persuade us by their opennesss and honesty who, when we are removed from their company, make us wonder: was not the inattention they managed to create in us towards the more petty and sordid side of life, itself a deception? I think particularly of the good, beautiful, generous wife of a suspicious, unloveable husband – a deeply wronged woman surely. And yet there may be terrible cruelty in the non-existence for her – which she communicates to me – of the things that loom so large in her jealous husband's eyes.

When someone is trying to persuade me how deeply he has been wronged, there is always one vital thing left out: the other person. He may constantly refer to her with genuine desire for understanding of her point of view. But another person's point of view is, at root, the other person: not anything that he or she may be *understood* to be claiming, but the claim that he *is* on life, by his very existence.

Each of us makes a case for himself. But each of us *is* a case. And no one's case, in that sense, gets or can get the consideration it deserves. The reason why the person from whom I seek this consideration cannot give it is his concern with *his own* case. And *that* is the one thing he cannot get consideration from *me* for! So that which withholds another from considering me is that which I cannot consider in him. That in me which leaves you alone in your tragedy is my tragedy.

This is not a picture of universal selfishness. It is simply a picture of selves together.

Each person is, of his nature, a magnetic field that distorts reality into its pattern. Each of us wants, and has to want, reality to be after the manner of his field. There is an appropriate loss of innocence which comes to see that, while the manipulation of others in its grosser and more cynical forms is to be deplored and curbed, a person-with-others is manipulative by nature. Each of us wants it his way. To cease altogether so to want it is to cease to be a person.

But I am also dissatisfied with having it my way. I experience that in *thus* having it my way I am not free. Language expresses this fact. For the tone of voice in which one says to a person 'have it your own way!' is a tone that *withholds* something. Verbally it gives freedom. In truth it withholds it. The most dishonest statements are those in which we give each other freedom. Permissive statements are dismissive statements.

What we more deeply seek from each other is another kind of permission: a permission to be myself, that is not simply a concession to my magnetic field, that does not consist in drawing an invisible ring round me and agreeing, inaudibly, not to encroach. Within that ring, I have no freedom. The only *climate* in which my freedom can flower is the climate that is constituted by, and consists of, other selves. And what we call a community is a being-together of people in which the *very thing* that imposed caution on my claim for myself and led me to lie to the other people about my claim – that is, other people with *their* claims – has managed somehow to become the climate, the warmth and moisture and sunlight, in which I live and make creative and self-revealing initiatives. Such extraordinary human phenomena exist, but they are rare.

The reason they are rare is that most people cannot afford them. I cannot afford to let you be yourself, to the extent that I cannot afford to relax *my* hold on reality, to turn off my magnetic field, to rid myself of that inner fear whose outward face is disapproval.

But this is not as simple as it sounds to some people. It is no problem at all to the hippie. He turns off the current with the utmost ease. There is in him no potential disapproval. *Anything* you do will meet with his open smile. And this, of course, is a cheat, and the person in you knows it. If anything goes, then you are part of 'anything'. He does not say, with the bourgeois, 'leave me alone and I'll leave you alone'. He says 'what's all this talk of leaving alone? There is no alone!' And there is. It is bloody. It is hideously hungry. It is vulnerable. Its name is man. Thinking to make a climate for it, the hippie makes a desert. It has been said by some who have experienced it that there is nothing quite so palpably empty as a place that the hippie community has left. San Francisco was like that when they moved on. This fever of instant love transformed our complicated species into a swarm of locusts.

The process whereby a person is transformed from the passionate hold on reality that he natively is into being a holding-ground for others, from merely *seeking*, to *being*, the bread of life, cannot be short-circuited.

I have to learn that my hold not only impedes your quest for life, but also impedes my own, as yours impedes yours. Correspondingly, it is not only your way of living that paralyzes my self-expression and says 'don't risk it!' My self-expression is impeded by *my* hold on reality. At the centre of the whole turmoil, in other words, is man in turmoil with himself. More specifically, it is what seems and must seem to me my thrust for freedom, my drive to live, that is the structure of my unfreedom. My hold on life is a strangle-hold. Can I release it?

It is at this point that Christianity makes a most extraordinary and ambitious statement. For first, it says, 'no, you can't, and stay a person. Your hold will relax only when you go through a total change.' But even that is easily said: it will be taken to refer simply to the *magnitude* of the operation. What is outlandish about Christianity is what it says of the *manner* of the operation.

For the operation consists in taking this self-destroying stance of man and arranging for it to *go much further*. It creates for the feared, ill-known, and repressed self of man a symbol – a symbol not taken simply from the world of dreams where certainly it acquires its symbolic status, but from the very history in which man hacks out his way: a symbol that, once it has shown itself as the very heart of the human, calls forth *all* the fear that is in man in the act of its destruction. More important, this showing is not, primarily, for man's *rebuke*. It is for his acting-out. It is designed to let him destroy his wholeness and *so* to discover the love that is the indestructability of that wholeness. Only in the power of a love stronger than himself in his passionate hold on being, can man live the community of man. And he comes under that power *only* by shooting his bolt, by exhausting his power for an ultimate and Godless selfhood.

The christian is a person who has shot his bolt as a person and found himself twice a person in the love of God. The identity that

41

slowly flows into him as he learns to live with the crucified, is the life which, while it properly bears his name, is the climate in which others are finding their growing.

Now this operation is of a wonderful psychological exactitude. Psychology has come to understand the value of the ego. While the study of depth psychology, unfolding as it did the riches that lie in the unconscious, was tempted to see as its task the weakening of the ego in favour of this superior source of life, a more mature and practised understanding has shown this policy to be disastrous. Somehow the power of the unconscious must be invoked in a manner that does not introduce doubt and wavering into the ego.

Now if I am asked to name a mystic exercise in which the ego would have full scope, I cannot think of a more dramatic example than the contemplation of Jesus crucified. For in that contemplation my ego becomes conscious of itself as the crucifier. It is no serene paradigm of human wholeness that is placed before me for my dreamy meditation, but the victim of the way I live. Mysterious though it is and has to be, the process whereby a person enters more and more into life as a necessary and forgiven crucifier of life, answers, to an incomparable degree, to the requirement of depth-psychology: that the ego undergo transformation yet maintain its proper vigour.

13   CONCUPISCENCE

In every important decision a person faces, there is, underlying the
clear question as to which course to pursue, the obscure question
'what sort of person do I want to become?' The underlying question,
for all its obscurity, points to the nature of freedom. At critical
moments, especially when one unbosoms to a close friend, the underlying question shows itself: we have an acute sense that that is
what is at stake, and that that is *why* this decision is momentous. But
this question is never without obscurity. Nor does it ever describe a
situation that we can totally master. *That* kind of description refers,
in the nature of things, to the clarities of the first question: shall I
take the job? *There* I am, in the common understanding, free. But at
the deeper level of the second question, my freedom is never in the
clear: and this precisely where my freedom is most real, most present, and most itself. This is the central paradox of freedom: where it
is most itself it is to a considerable extent unrealised. Where my
freedom most truly is, is where it is only *trying* to happen.

It is trying to happen, trying to be, *in* that ongoing process that is
my life. That thrust goes ahead inexorably, however conscious or
unconscious we may be in it. I am a complex and, in a sense,
well-run household, a whole complex of systems dedicated to my
survival. It is well-run in the sense that it will keep going, somehow,
in whatever circumstances. Karl Rahner calls this my 'spontaneity'.
And he means by 'concupiscence' this spontaneity *in so far as* it is
working on its own and not as the implementation of my freedom. It
works thus on its own to a considerable extent in all of us, to a
markedly lesser extent in a holy, whole person, but still to a significant extent in all men and women.

How does this concupiscence relate to evil? It is not itself a
proneness to evil. Evil is not *in* my concupiscence, but in the fact that

it is not with my freedom but going its own way. Evil, in other words, is the lack of wholeness, of all-togetherness. It consists in the fact that my freedom is confined to the sphere of my decisions, of whether I take that job or not: my freedom in taking the job does not realise itself much at the deeper level at which the question 'what sort of person do I want to become?' poses itself. In taking that job, I shall in fact be defining to a further extent the sort of person I am becoming. But how much do I have to do with that becoming? How much do I carve myself in the job that carves me? *That* is what is meant by the question 'how free am I?' That is what is asked by the question 'how free am I?'

We might clarify this by distinguishing between 'my freedom in decision' and 'my freedom *under* the decision'. In so far as my freedom in decision does not penetrate to the level of my spontaneity, we have the 'concupiscent' situation. I am free in respect of the job, pretty unfree in respect of myself – and, as I have said, it is there that I most need to be free and that freedom really *is* freedom.

Evil, I repeat, is not *in* my spontaneity but in the out-of-phase-ness of my spontaneity with my freedom. With these two out of phase, *neither* is necessarily better or worse than the other. *Either* may be on the side of the angels. Thus, if my spontaneity is heading towards a destructive relationship, my decision to go against my spontaneity and not enter the relationship will be the right decision, and in this case it is my decision-part that is on the side of the angels. But on the other hand, I might, in an important matter, decide to lie. In the act of lying, I blush violently and give myself away. In *this* case, it is my spontaneity that is on the right side. But in neither of these two cases do we have integral goodness. We have only a partial attainment of the good: in one case, by my decision, with my spontaneity left out in the cold (and please God it will *get* cold!): in the other case, by my spontaneity, with my decision-part exposed to shame. And the *radical* evil in these two situations lies not in my spontaneous proneness to adultery but in the fact that my *avoidance* of adultery is not with my whole being: not in my deliberate lie but in the fact that I *can* act with only part of myself.

Luther says that all men are disobedient to the Law of God, because the Law of God requires obedience from the heart, and 'concupiscent' man *cannot* give obedience (a decision) from the heart (man's total spontaneity).

44

This is the meaning of Paul's statement in Romans, that the Law is spiritual but man is of the flesh. 'Spiritual' means 'addressed to the whole man', 'requiring obedience from the heart'. 'Fleshly' means 'not *being* a whole man'. Man the divided cannot respond adequately to God who requires man the whole. Thus it is a misunderstanding of this text to say that the part of man that *can* obey, the decision-part, is the good and spiritual part, the spontaneity that doesn't go along with this obedience the bad and unspiritual part. There is no 'good *part*' of a person, for good is of the whole: it is in non-togetherness of the parts that the evil of man consists.

God seeks from man, as alone appropriate, the movement of his whole being, his life: that is to say, he seeks man's praise.

Thus we have to think of integrity or human wholeness as that condition in which the sphere of personal choice, more precisely of self-disposal, is co-extensive with and is expressed in the whole world of a person's natural movements and spontaneities. A condition for which, in Jungian terms, there is no more 'unconscious'. Such a condition is not the human condition as we know it, although it consists in the harmony of two parts of man that are clearly meant to be in harmony. When they come into a partial harmony in a person, all but the perversely unpeaceful recognise in that person the figure of the wise and desirable man.

Now traditional scholastic theology said a very surprising thing about the state of freedom from concupiscence. Although the state of non-freedom was obviously a sickness, an unwholeness – with the implication that the cognate wholeness would be a 'natural perfection' – traditional theology said that freedom from concupiscence was a preternatural gift of God, not a perfection of the kind that the Creator 'owes' to the creature by reason of the latter's divinely founded essence. In other words, it conceived of man as by nature sick!

I believe that this idea was an inspired guess. The dividedness of man between self-disposing 'person' and spontaneous 'nature' is the most radical one we know. The varieties of its dialectic are endless. Its power to queer the pitch in human relations is likewise endless. By this analysis we are lightyears beyond the picture of man as having a 'good' side that tends to God and an 'evil' side that tends away from him.

Consider the case of a person who freely decides to seek and to do

45

God's will but who encounters violent opposition to this decision in the sphere of his spontaneous desires. Now the customary simplistic analysis of this situation says that the above description *is* its analysis, with the will for God, concupiscence against him. In reality these spontaneous desires not only militate against the free decision for God, but make that decision the poorer and the less Godly by their absence from the dominion of the will. The temptation I have to resist contains a vital element of the goodness in whose name I resist it.

I recently described my life as 'divided between men in search of life and half-men in search of God.' That is a rather vivid description of the state that is not free of concupiscence: not free, that is, of the great human separation of powers, of will and appetite. This separation appears equally in my pious friends whose pursuit of God leaves out so much of human appetite, and in my impious ones whose appetites forever postpone that discipline in which alone they can flower and improve the human condition.

I have spoken earlier of man as resisting the fulness of personhood to which God is calling him. I have depicted Jesus as the symbol of this wholeness, and of his crucifixion as the bringing out into the open of man's resistance to becoming whole. Now what Rahner has pinpointed is the *structure* of man's refusal. The refusal of God's call to wholeness is the tendency of decision and spontaneity to stay apart. We prefer them apart. Faced with any decision, we strive to leave part of ourselves out of it. We resist a temptation, but we keep it going. We make a decision, but we look for the escape clause. Nothing is final in this life – and by God we want it that way. We are inveterate two-timers. I absolutely dread the thought of the whole of me coming together in a 'yes' to somebody or something, with nothing of myself left out, and therefore no possibility of retreat. Yes, I *want* it too, I know. Sometimes I sort of feel for it in prayer. But the dread and the desire are inextricably intertwined.

Christianity is revolutionary. For it makes the death of Christ reconciliatory in the sense of making *God* convincing to *us*, of displacing for us the God of our fear. It makes it clear that it was *only* a question of opening *our minds and hearts* for God to appear. No question of placating *God*. It refers to the miraculous cessation of fear, and the consequent appearance of a totally new God, no longer the God we have seen filtered through the human nightmare.

But this revision requires prolonged and sustained meditation, really to appreciate how much is involved of our whole approach to religion and to its connection with our human relations.

How very much of our natural and customary religious thinking is going in the direction of placating *God*. It will be worthwhile to make this overt at different levels.

First, at the level of formal theology, theologians affirm that there is no question of placating God in the literal sense, as in pagan sacrifices. But as regards how the propitiatory sacrifice of Christ works, there is a mass of conflicting theories. And the whole thing is said to be 'mysterious' which, in the context of clearing God of bloodthirsty sentiments, makes us suspicious. We have a right to expect a clear statement as to why this sacrifice is not a placating of God: namely, that it is a placating, a pacifying, *of us* about God or to let God in. In the usual theological account, *the direction* of the movement *from us to God* remains unchanged, with the vague qualification that the normal function of a bloody sacrifice is somehow modified. In fact, the point that theologians describe as mysterious is embarrassingly simple – like the sudden discovery that a person who seemed to me to be behaving in a most extraordinary way is in fact in love with me.

Secondly, at the ethical level, we call upon the experience that tells us that the arrival at truth is a painful and costing affair, and so see the Passion of Christ as a striking example of this. Our model is Pelagian, making of the agony of Christ the supreme example of 'getting there at the cost of blood'. Once again, the *direction* in which we are thinking if 'from us to God'. Jesus 'made it' – for us of course, though how this act of monumental stoicism is 'for us' remains unclear.

Thirdly, at the more primitive level, which is still potently operative in us, where we think of religion as a series of attempts to win God's favour, the sacrifice of Christ goes into a practical osmosis with all the dodges we use to this end. Once again, the direction is 'from us to God', is a matter of 'us getting there'.

Now this direction, which is presupposed at all these levels, intellectual, moral, and primitive, *is reversed*. Not modified, not substituted for by some *other* way, not *getting further* than the pagan sacrifices, but reversed.

Once the thing has thus been thrown into reverse, we find ourselves beginning to think of God in a new way. We have to think of a God closer to our evil than we ever dare to be. We have to think of him not as standing at the end of the way we take when we run *away* from our evil in the search for good, but as taking hold of us *in* our evil, at the sore point which the whole idealistic thrust of man is concerned to avoid.

Let us now ask *why* the spontaneous and inertial direction of our thought is 'from us to God'.

The answer, already implied, is that the animal, become conscious, is impelled *away* from its centre as a being at once self-aware and at the mercy of total process, to fashion an ideal, a projection, an ennobled existence able to forget its frightening contingency. *All* that it dreams up in this desperate enterprise, all its institutions, all its symbols, all its power-figures, all its gods, *even its image of the one God,* are functions of this great movement *away* from the centre *towards* the ideal. Thus the religious quest, whether we view it in the propitiatory sacrifice of the Incas or in the intellectual and moral strivings of Plotinus, is 'trying to get there', 'trying to make it'. The religious dream is the dream of man's self-ennobling, of man's achievement of meaning, as at last 'coming off'. And when, through the Mosaic and subsequent revelation, there is engrafted into this dream a belief in the one God who is transcendent, and when, final-

48

ly, we learn that union with this transcendent Being has been achieved through the death of the Son of Man, millennia of psychic habit in us hear this as meaning that at last the transcendent God has looked down and said 'OK, you made it, I am satisfied.' Redemption through the blood of Christ is interpreted as the bending of Reality itself to man's great dream of himself.

And it is exactly the reverse. It is the ending of the dream. It is the beautiful collapse of the whole enterprise. It is the invasion of man by himself, with God at the centre as love.

All this sounds theoretical. But its import is embarrassingly practical. For the implication is, that just in so far as our religious mind is operating normally, God's making of love on the cross should appear to us as pathetic. It *is* pathetic. It is *in* the pathetic. It is in the unbearable place.

For man who seeks it in the place of his nobility, his sublimity, the Absolute is in the pathetic.

The revelation of God's love in the Passion of Christ is far more like the embarrassing and happy discovery that someone is simply in love with us than our mind is *capable* of reconciling with the way we still *have* to think of God. Those moments of revelation between two people are temporary and blessed reversals in man's flight from himself. The cross of Jesus, looked at with faith, is the total and final reversal.

But this total and final reversal takes place in the context of the people we are, still conscious animals scared of our animality and seeking to ennoble ourselves. Still only able to survive in this way. In other words there is a tension here that will only be resolved in the Parousia. And this means that our normal humanity, with all its interpreted experience, is always in the position of being surprised by the humble, pathetic, and kind of ordinary nature of God's love in Christ. Meditation is a discipline, which each of us must discover in the way most suited to him or her, for increasing the frequency of these moments of surprise. A Jesuit retreat-giver created one of these moments by pointing to the crucifix and saying 'What a way to run a universe!' The vision of the crucified is a huge therapeutic interruption of the struggle to survive. St. Paul says 'God was in Christ, reconciling the world to himself.' Try, in this text, to hear God saying 'I am in the Man you are destroying in your search for me.'

In Shakespeare's play 'A Comedy of Errors' each character is mistaken as to other characters' identity and intentions. In the dénouement, all is discovered to the happiness of all. Man's whole religious history is a comedy of errors. Its dénouement is on Calvary. But this dénouement takes place at the heart of a still darkened world. It is for the empowering of saints with the laughter that will in the end save the world.

15 A PRECISION

'You contradict yourself', someone will say, 'for at one time you speak of man as self-crucifying, at another as self-loving, self-worshipping, self-absorbed.'

But what we are trying to look at is 'man without God', the most powerful self-contradiction there can be.

Of course man is never without God. But in Christ man is *with* God so wholly, that this condition demands for its full understanding a correspondingly rigorous idea of man without God. The Christian fact generates of necessity the possibility of its absence. It is in the nature of a master switch that, thrown, would plunge the world into a fearsome darkness.

Looking, then, at the *logic* of 'man without God', we see him saying to his life 'you're all I've got' – and do we not know from experience what a threat to the beloved lurks in that style of love-profession? In fact, this act of self-worship sets the limitless miracle of man's life on a pedestal where it becomes limited, a possession, an asset. So the underside of the worship of humanity is its paralyzing, its immobilizing. The inner meaning of self-worship is self-crucifixion.

Part Two

THE DEAD AND RISEN

1 EVEN UNTO DEATH

Hitherto we have considered only the dynamic of *the crucifixion*. And we have concentrated on this dynamic as it happens in the experience of the believer. Now the death of Jesus *as a process he undergoes* has not entered into the building-up of the dynamic. The dynamic is one of confrontation, consciousness raising, sorrow, healing, and self-discovery. Central to this dynamic is the death of Jesus *as caused by sin*, but not the death of Jesus *as a process he undergoes*. That is the *extension* of the dynamic, not a primary ingredient in it.

This distinction is vital. This book can be summed up in one sentence: His death caused by sin is our life. His death caused by sin is salvation. The confrontation between man the sinner and Jesus crucified is how salvation happens. The mistake is to miss or blur this foundational idea, and then to speak of Jesus' death *as a process* which is, in prototype, the salvation of man. This is the mistake of putting, in the place of the victim who mediates the forgiveness of sin, the hero who, in our name, breaks through death to new life.

Jesus does break the power of death for us. But the *power* of death – as opposed to the *fact* of death – is due to sin, and so Jesus breaks this power by mediating the forgiveness of sin. There simply is no other way to break it.

Given this, the death of Jesus as process becomes meaningful. The death of Jesus can then *only* appear as process, and not as the enigma and tragedy that death in our world is. What I now want to say depends wholly on getting this order right: *first*, sin and its resolution; *then*, the symbolism of death.

Why did we get this order wrong? Why did we get fed up with the sin-business and meditating on Jesus on the cross? I shall only speak for myself. I lacked the maturity to see sin as self-crucifixion. I did not have anything in my psyche to *see* in Jesus on the cross. I think that's why, having had that experience in the Italian church, I promptly forgot it.

The evil preference for unwholeness is the desire for death. Preeminently it is the desire for the death of Jesus who represents the whole man.

But 'evil desirous of the death of Jesus' is evil on the verge of redemption. This is the ultimate mystery of us: that even our evil, even our tendency against wholeness, exposes us to the love of God. And it exposes us to that love in a way and at a depth to which even our desire for wholeness does not expose us. This is the psychological reason for the dogmatically clichéd statement that only by the blood of Jesus are we saved, only by his stripes are we healed. Jung insists that evil has to enter into our integration, and charges Christianity with leaving it out. Jung is right about evil. It has to enter. In an unfathomable way it *desires* its own transformation. But evil enters into the total transformation only through crucifying Jesus.

Note
It is only in a world in which freedom and spontaneity have become synonymous that the redeemed condition would be adequately *defined* as one of freedom. That is not the world of our experience. Thus the 'freedom' of the new creation may only be hinted at. It is conveyed through image and symbol rather than conceptually. The mysterious thing about this freedom is, that it is *at once*, and in one miraculous and total transformation, the freeing of will from the enslavement of desire and the freeing of desire from its enslavement by will.

55

2 THE DEATH OF THE LORD

What a fuss we make about death! The way we think about death is the extreme case of the ego's habit of characterising a larger reality, of which it is part, by its effect on itself. 'Fog in the Channel. Continent Isolated.', a 19th century English headline read. If we could be observed by some being from outer space who was perfectly integrated into the life process, he would say: 'These humans regard their re-entry into the life-cycle exclusively as an event happening to *them*. They seem to have some *other* thing going for them than life, and they understand death not as part of the life-process but as the cessation *of that other thing*. Thus they speak of the death of their great men as though it were a great misfortune, a turn of ill-luck, that should not have happened. It is very difficult to convey what *they* mean by "death".'

We turn away from our animal involvement in the life-process, and throw our best energies into doing those things that with death will simply cease. We have our ego, and then death has its, and its is the last word. And thus we confer on death the quality of victory, a quality it does not have of itself. As though the water were to say, on reaching what *we* see simply as boiling-point, 'the fire has conquered'. Instead of being a moment in the process, death for us is the breakdown of the attempt to live eternally and in despite of the process. And since the attempt to live eternally and to constitute reality for ourselves is that arrogation of divinity that is called sin, death for us is the penalty of sin.

Further, death regarded in this way is an isolated event. It is the end of your thing. It is the end of my thing. There is nothing so isolated as the way in which each person tries to centre the world on himself, tries to constitute his own reality. In other words there is nothing so isolated as what our galactic observer sees each human as

56

doing 'besides living', which *we* see death as the ending of. And so, correspondingly, there is nothing so alone as the death which terminates each man's 'thing that he does'.

And so death, viewed from the standpoint of the ego, has two qualities. It is the victory over meaning as we try to secure it. And it is an isolated event. These two are complementary. For the absolutely isolated event is by definition the event without meaning.

Another effect of the ego-perspective is that death becomes as it were personified. What for the galactic observer is simply the point of re-entry into cosmic process is for the human the Great Event. Our ego-operations are so important that what brings them to an end is correspondingly important. It is a Thing in its own right. 'It' triumphs when in fact all that has happened is the re-entry of an animal into the life-process. Of the universal process in which things come to be and pass back into the process, the humans have their peculiar version, according to which *I* manage to get something done and then 'Death' triumphs. Thus the reification of death reflects the illusory centrality of the ego.

Now in Jesus we honour the man without sin, the man without private building. In contemplating his death we are forced to see human death in its primary meaning, as re-entry into the process.

But because Jesus is not a *regression* to the innocent animal state but an *advance* into further consciousness, this purely processive nature of death, which he realises through sinlessness, is a 'return to the Father'. The symbolism of return to the Father is heavy with meaning and healing beauty. It is experienced by us as a huge deculturalisation of death, a lifting of its heavy sombre symbolism, a cleansing.

But how are we, children of culture, to appropriate this new symbolism of death? Death for us remains laden with its human meaning. How can we celebrate this primary death? For symbolism is not changed by an act of understanding. Symbolism is only changed by a radical shift in experience.

Remember that it is sin that confers on death its *old* symbolism. Sin is the constituting of our own reality as *the* reality, making of death the ultimate victory. Now we have seen, in the figure of the Crucified, the destruction of our larger reality made overt for us, and thus overt, toppling over into the all-embracing love of God. We have experienced, in this vision of the Crucified, the forgiveness of

57

our sin. And *thus* we are liberated from the old, sinful vision of death and enabled to see our victim in his death as 'returning to the Father'. The Father whose infinite embrace receives us sinners receives in that same embrace, and as the focus of our new vision, our bleeding victim. In acknowledging ourselves as sinners, we find our identity in the man our sin has crucified, and in him, know death as the Father's embrace.

That is why our Paschal liturgy constantly invokes, for the validity of its great image of the Lord's passage to the Father, the resolution of our sin in the crucifixion. That is why the Hero of the Exultet is he who 'by his holy blood paid Adam's and our debt.'

I have said that death, understood within the limits of culture, is a meaningless, isolated event. At the opposite pole is the death of Jesus which is universal in scope, being what death, regardless of culture, is for man. But we come into this universal scope only through the forgiveness of our sin, because it is our sin that makes death the ruler, and will continue to do so until it has found its resolution in the love of God.

This bears out one of the main convictions of this book: the anthropology of the New Testament, of the new man, only falls into place when it is centred on the forgiveness of sin: more precisely, centred on the Crucified, the mirror-image of sin, which offers to those who look into it forgiveness.

But this also means, conversely, that in order fully to appropriate and celebrate our condition of forgiven people we need to exercise ourselves in the contrast between the death of Jesus as a liturgical fact and death as our culture mourns it, for this contrast is the full symbolic extension of the contrast between the regenerate and the unregenerate condition. As a theme for meditation, ask yourself what sort of a funeral you'd give Jesus. Have some fun with this. How about a slap-up affair, with gun-carriages and a gun salute? Then you might suddenly realise what an extraordinary man you've got on your hands and in your heart. The medieval Church got pretty close to the gun-carriage when it celebrated Good Friday *in black*! A deviation itself oddly instructive.

We are thinking of that cultural misfit, a death that *means* 'return to the Father'. One of the things our theology most needs is a tightening up on the handling of symbolism. For how many theologians and spiritual writers, for instance, is not Jesus' self-oblation on a cross simply the exemplar of the 'holy death'? The category invoked is 'death as we know it, but made by a holy person the occasion for the ultimate act of surrender to God.' *In* that category, Jesus is supreme. The *symbolism* of death remains unchanged. Whereas in reality the symbolism of death is here broken open. This is the meaning of 'dying you destroyed our death.' *Our* 'death'. What we have made death into. He who contemplates the death of the Lord enters a new world. Or rather he enters into the hitherto unexplored depth of *this* world, in the penetrating power of the Spirit. And this is why the death of Jesus is a theme for celebration independently of the Eucharist that is its celebration. The Eucharist *grows out of* the death of the Lord, implementing the latter's inherently celebratory character.

3   THE END OF THE JOURNEY IN SIGHT

The real meaning of Jesus' death is a meaning purely of consummation.

Now this 'meaning of consummation' is, at one and the same time, the clearing of death of its heavy cultural symbolism, its ego-centred tragic quality, and the full flowering of the victim in his power to absorb and transform our evil. As the full development of the victim, his death takes us deeper into the forgiveness experience, since this latter is the subjective component in our vision of the victim. And thus Jesus, in his transformation of 'our death', perfects in us the forgiveness experience. The believer's eyes are opened to a world unclouded by culture-qualified ego-centred death *not* through some cosmic ideology but through the experience of forgiveness in its completed state. It is the deep, labyrinthine, complex and evil-complicated heart of man that has to be opened for the new world to appear. The cosmic Christ, the Christ that death liberates, is the Christ who conveys the message of forgiveness to the depths of the human heart and so makes it cosmic not just civic. It is *as* this finality of forgiveness and divine presence that he *appears* 'in the glory of God the Father'.

To the believer, to man-in-forgiveness, this death is *joyful*, in a human world in which death cannot by wholly joyful. And finally this death is *glorious* with the glory of another world, the real world of God.

Thus, while scriptural exegesis distinguishes two great themes or motifs of redemption, namely expiation and passage out of this world to the Father, these are only two dimensions of one Christian experience. Endlessly they interpenetrate. For the way beyond this world – this human culture-defined world – to the Father is the way of forgiveness. The victim who awakens and accuses sin and resolves it in forgiveness, the man who deculturalises death and makes it a passage beyond this world, and the son who is in the glory of the Father, are one and the same symbol, mediating one same experience of liberation.

As the victim dies and changes 'our death', we see further into the victim out of a deeper experience of forgiveness: and in seeing him in his end, in the glory of the Father, we know the complete form of that experience.

As sin in us has as its full extension 'our death', so precisely does sin's victim have as *his* full extension a death that is return to the Father. And as 'our death' is the perfect symbol of sin in us, so the consummated victim is the perfect symbol of our forgiveness. As the school of humanistic introspection teaches us to see further and further into our death out of further and further reaches of our futility, so the school of the cross teaches us to see further and further into the victim out of further and further reaches of our forgiveness.

The unity of the two redemptive themes, of expiation and passage, is the heart of an integral Christian experience. Jesus does not take us to the Father by going on that journey as our representative and carrying us along with him by throwing out sacramental lifelines. Jesus goes to the Father in our experience of him as victim, which is our experience of ourselves as forgiven and cut loose from our self-made world. 'I ascend to my Father and your Father; to my God and your God.' His exaltation as victim, completing as it does the forgiveness of our sin-captive and culture-bounded heart, puts us at last in the liberated condition in which God can *be* God. The passionate and total experience of God as Father which makes Jesus the victim of narcissistic and fearful man, is given to man in the forgiveness that the victim mediates.

It is, then, seriously misguided to advocate a shift of emphasis from the 'old-fashioned' Jesus-on-the-cross-for-sin approach to the 'more positive' theme of the Paschal Mystery, the passage of Jesus to the Father. 'The Paschal Mystery' being the full development of the mystery of sin and forgiveness through the victim, a failure to grasp this latter will be enlarged in the picture we form of the Paschal Mystery. This picture will be a hotch-potch of myth and cheery optimism: an even worse insult to the heart than the dreary old meditations on the Passion.

With the contemplation of Jesus *dead* on the cross, our journey into the crucifix comes to its end. While 'Jesus crucified' has raised the whole issue of sin and dictated the dynamic of salvation, 'Jesus dead' raises the issue of sin's anthropological extension, that is to say, 'our death', and dictates the full extension of the above dynamic into a new anthropology with death as passage and God as God. And this final vision of the crucified is the Trinitarian theophany. The Holy Spirit in this theophany is the fully extended subjective dimension upon which the objective vision of the victim and his glory in the Father increasingly depends. The Holy Spirit weds the man on the cross to the forgotten and emergent self of the believer, and thus enables him to see his salvation in a joyful and cosmic death into the glory of God the Father.

4 JESUS JOINS THE FATHER IN THE HEART OF THE BELIEVER

The expression 'perfect conformity to the will of God' is the overwhelmingly preferred description of 'Christian perfection.' It means a loving acceptance of whatever God may send, and that 'whatever' can be genuinely open-ended. It thus includes 'death, accepted purely as the will of God.'

But what it gives no hint of, is that even man with Christ in so far as he thinks of himself naturally and still has to think of himself if he is to live in this human world, *is not capable* of accepting death 'purely as the will of God.' Death for him is 'our death', the tragic and enigmatic downfall of the anti-god, of the ego-centred consciousness. It is the enemy.

Thus the spiritual axiom of total conformity to the will of God has to *presuppose* that massive transformation of death by Christ that is the central Christian mystery. And mysteries are not meant to be presupposed. They have to be named, to school the mind and heart, and to be celebrated. Only in the context of this faith, contemplation and celebration, and as a comment on it, is the axiom of perfect conformity to God's will adequate to the new life. It is either a paschal axiom, or it is inadequate to the new condition.

It is not understood as such by spiritual writers. For the tendency is for it to create its own mental world, thus generating as the symbol of perfection the image of a man, within the world as we experience and interpret it, totally accepting the will of God. Christ thus appears merely as the most perfect example of this type of obedience.

In reality, his is that unique obedience to which death is not 'our death' but the gift of the Father. 'Death as the Father's gift, as the Father's love in action' is the prerogative of Christ. And it is only by virtue of assimilation to him through the forgiveness of the depth of our being, that it is ours.

But we cannot speak of assimilation to Christ without considering him as he is now. His present condition is implied in the fact that his death 'destroys our death'. I mean, that the corollary of 'dying you destroyed our death' is 'dead you are not among our dead.' Let us examine this proposition

There is an immediate and necessary connection between the way we, in our self-alienated condition, see death, and the way we think of the dead. 'Think' is not an adequate word. It is rather a question of the way the human psyche experiences the dead. This is reflected in all the great literature in which the psyche finds expression, and in all the great myths of man.

Remember our galactic observer. He said 'these humans see death not as a moment in a process, understood in reference to the process, but as the solemn end of something they have temporarily snatched from the process.'

It might be thought that the dead would exist for us no more. What happens is almost the contrary of this. Our sense of death, which we repress when we think of ourselves, our life, and its opportunities, finds its outlet in the way we view the dead.

The death that we will not allow to have *any* hold on us, we see as having a *total* hold on the dead. All the unknowness in life, that militates against our ego-centred building, we invest in the dead. We cannot bear to think of *ourselves* as but part of the total mystery, so we think of *them* in this way. They are the alibi for our sense of death.

This constitutes a deep divide, a gulf, between the living and the dead: between the living who are *without* mystery and the dead who are *saturated* with it.

This divide, carried to its extreme, becomes meaninglessness. For then the dead are defined as 'not living' and the living defined as 'not dead'.

We are moved away from this extreme by poets like Rilke and the later D. H. Lawrence, who raise up the dead as the accusers of our shallowness. In James Joyce's short story 'The Dead' the not-so-young bride recalls a long-dead young lover on one of the first nights of her marriage. Although the relationship was not a serious one, the husband feels it would be an intrusion to sleep with her. Going to the window and looking out at the falling snow, he feels *all* the dead rising against him, accusing from nameless depths the vulgarity of his ego.

It is not only these works of literature that tend to topple our safe view of ourselves and of the dead 'in their place'. Ira Progoff says that people he has treated have had most fruitful dialogues with dead parents, and I have proved this in my own experience.

Nevertheless, the divide that we make between the living and the dead, though open to criticism and partial correction, is as incorrigible as sin: and, like sin, it looks not to *correction* but to *redemption,* a radical transformation. And indeed, even our more significant and more human experience of the dead tends to emphasize in its way the divide. There is a solemnity about the dialogue that smacks of our self-centred, humourless, Godless condition.

In blazing contrast with our world of the dead, with our Sheol, our Hades, our séances, our shades is the fact that Jesus, whose death exposes and invalidates 'our death', *is therefore not among our dead.*

Of course the statement 'Christ is risen' is up for grabs. You can have him stepping out of the tomb. You can have him stepping out of whatever Sheol or Hades you locate the dead in. Or you can understand the statement in a 'purely spiritual' sense to refer to the abiding truth of his message. But the most radical understanding contrasts Christ's condition with what the dead are for sinful man.

We can make the following rule for New Testament interpretation, in this matter of the Resurrection. That interpretation of 'the Lord is risen' is closest to the heart of the New Testament that understands it as flowing most immediately out of his conquest of sin. As the fullest understanding of man's plight is that man is sinner, so the fullest understanding of the Redeemer in his completed condition is that which sees this as the full radiation of his overcoming sin. Thus 'risen from the dead' means 'not among our dead as they are for us sinners.'

Of course there is a linguistic difficulty here. For 'risen from the dead' means that he *was* dead and then ceased to be dead. But could not the initial resurrection experience be the change *of the disciples* from experiencing him as dead to experiencing him as not among the dead? This would mean that the resurrection experience was their changing from the condition of sinners into the new condition of the redeemed. And this is what the resurrection experience has been in the Church and its liturgy ever since. It is the total experience of release from sin. We see, in the New Testament itself, the progressive deepening of the interpretation: starting at 'an event that happened to Jesus after he was dead', we arrive at the Johannine picture of resurrection as the direct emanation of Christ's salvific nature.

The image of Jesus burns in the soul of the believer with a fire which burns up his underworld, the extended creation of his pathetic self-sufficiency.

In our dead we see the life that we try to *ignore* and forever *postpone*. We see the mystery that we *evade*. In Jesus, on the other hand, we see this mysterious wholeness *not* as we evade it but as we *crucify* it. We see it, in other words, in the most radical form of our dialogue with it, the drama of sin and its forgiveness. And thus in Jesus the mysterious wholeness of our life comes upon us and engulfs us with an immediacy that the dead cannot have. That in us which banishes the dead cannot banish him who undermines it.

We cannot receive from the dead him whose death never placed him there but speaks to our sin as its dissolution along with our death. Jesus is a mystery of total consciousness in which the dead fall away, and are drawn into the new totality.

We have had him and we have him, too close to the centre of our being, ever to lose him in death. We have had him, and we have him, thus close, because in him we crucify our self, are at issue with our self, and can find resolution only in forgiveness. And this vast mystery of forgiveness binds into one the world of man that sin has broken into the two worlds of the living and the dead. And how can we honour him who reunites all the worlds, if we will persist in a theology that still tinkers with those worlds and leads its Redeemer through their labyrinthine and man-made ways?

We should meditate persistently on the difference between 'a victory of the life that we deny' and 'a return from the life that we have lost.'

We should ask ourselves what we are to make of a death that is not the denial of a life that is the denial of death! What makes all this so confusing, and generates such a morass of semantic problems about 'life' and 'death', is – the presence of the Father! With this death he is here. This death is him here. And how can the death that brings the Father allow any problem to arise as to where the Son has gone?

The trouble is that we have no language for a human life that does

66

not deny death. I mean, we can have no *word* for it, no *image* of it. Yet this is the reality that comes upon us in Christ. We negotiate it as best we can. And the best we can is to work out of our radical diagnosis of ourselves as sinners.

Note

It may help to set the foregoing ideas in a more overtly psychological pattern.

The psyche of man contains, or internalises, all reality, It has its heaven, its earth, and its underworld. Its earth is peopled by the people we know. Its underworld is peopled by the dead. Its heaven is peopled by heroes — the 'great dead' — and angels.

But also, the psyche has a *centre*. And the full task of the ego, which naturally thinks of itself as the centre, is to come into full appeasement with the centre.

Now the centre, *by its position,* is alive to, and coordinates, the three worlds of heaven, earth, and underworld. And thus he who represents or symbolizes the centre, Jesus Christ, belongs to all three worlds, of earth, of underworld, and of heaven, *but by being the centre.* Thus he is not *located* in any, either the earth, or heaven, or the world of the dead. It is on this basis that we say that he is 'not among the dead'. He 'knows', 'has tasted' death, but by reason of his centrality. It is thus that the converted ego begins to know and to experience him — not in any of the psyche's worlds but at its centre, and as its essential life.

But if we are to understand the nature of this converted experience of the centre, we have to ask *how* the ego comes into it.

The answer of the gospel has two components. On the one hand, it maintains that the centre is not only that which coordinates the worlds, but is the place of *transcendence,* of surrender to the infinite power that contains and transcends all that is or can ever be. On the other hand, and just *because* of this pressure of the infinite, the gospel's way of human centring is mysterious, crucial, and humanly demanding. Thus the gospel sees the drama of the ego's relationship to the centre as a drama of crucifixion, sorrow, and forgiveness. And *this* drama of centring *is* the opening of the centre to the infinite. Forgiveness is the power of the infinite pouring in to the centre.

Now we can bring together the meaning of Jesus as the centre, 'not among the dead', and the mystery of crucifixion, sorrow and forgiveness, and say: Jesus is not among the dead, Jesus is *thus* experienced by the converted ego, *because* he has been really experienced as centre *in the mystery of crucifixion and forgiveness*.

Finally, the centre *thus* known opens to the infinite. Jesus, dead but not among the dead, is with the Father. The mystery of crucifixion and forgiveness, that alone draws the ego definitively in to the centre where Jesus is experienced as filling all the worlds and not *among* 'the living' or 'the dead' or 'the great dead', opens out to the infinite.

Hence the scandalous simplicity of the gospel. Jesus can say 'if you have forgiven your brother from the heart, you are with the Father for ever. The whole mystery of the cross is active in you.'

5 NARCISSUS MAN

In 'The Denial of Death' Ernest Becker writes: 'One of the key concepts for understanding man's urge to heroism is the idea of narcissism. As Erich Fromm has so well reminded us, this idea is one of Freud's great and lasting contributions. Freud discovered that each of us repeats the tragedy of the mythical Greek Narcissus: we are hopelessly absorbed with ourselves.'

This self-absorption is to the degree of 'hopelessness'. An immediate intuition knows that it is fatal. This intuition finds its welcome expression in the Narcissus myth. But in order to let the myth speak fully in us, it is necessary to do all we can to appreciate, apart from the myth and before we sail into it, the logic that ties self-absorption to self-extinction.

What then is the logical connection between self-absorption and death?

In the first place, self-absorption is the movement of the flight from death. It is the huge desperate choice, by consciousness, of itself alone as against the surrounding world that threatens to absorb it. Man's self-absorption is his choice of self-awareness as against his animality. It is the desperate and unavoidable choice of only one of the two poles of his existence. So self-absorption is the flight from death. Where man flees from death is into himself.

But in thus choosing himself alone, man is opting for an ultimate solitude. This choice can be made not only by the individual as the unconscious structure of his desperation, but also by the whole human race. It *is* being made by the whole human race, as between the two poles, taking seriously only our self-awareness, ignoring our being-part-of, that is the ecology in whose balance we are partly animals. The human race thinks it can go on with all its Narcissistic human normalities, of war, of politics, of religion, and that somehow the vast *other* side of the picture will look after itself. So in opting for 'himself as conscious', man is opting for an ultimate solitude.

And ultimate solitude is death. It is to be cut off from the tree of life, and to wither.

And thus by a paradox that is built into the nature of conscious being, man realizes as spiritual isolation what is in any case his lot as animal. In his very flight from death he reinforces its hold upon him, making of it a spiritual hold. His flight from death accentuates it by making for himself a spiritual version of it. And whereas nature merely decrees death as part of her personal process, her bizarre creature man chooses death under the more awesome description: alone forever.

This is what is meant by the scripture's description of man as 'under the shadow of death'. It does not mean 'man knowing he will die' but 'what man *does* and *becomes* under this knowledge'. It is not to our mortality, our animality, that scripture offers a remedy. It is to the death that we become in our self-absorption. It is to what we allow death to become in us by fleeing from it in the hopeless pride of man.

Finally, some images from Eliot, to our purpose:

Those who sharpen the teeth of the dog, meaning Death
Those who glitter with the glory of the humming-bird, meaning
Death
Those who sit in the sty of contentment, meaning
Death
Those who suffer the ecstasy of the animals, meaning
Death

(From the poem *Marina*)

6 INTENSIFYING THE VISION AGAIN

In Jesus on the cross, I see the man I dare not be, dying the death I dare not die. Rather than be him I kill him. But my attempt to eliminate him confronts me with the perfect symbol of the death that I fear to die.

Jesus enfleshes for me the identity, the personhood, that I fear. Acting out this fear, and killing him, I confront myself with the very reason for my fear: the death that I dare not die.

The awful secret is that 'the man I dare not be' and 'the death I dare not die' are one and the same thing. My violent reaction to the first only confronts me with the second.

There is an indissoluble connection at the heart of our being, between death and the real person. But so hugely resistant are we to this connection, so wholly built is our culture, layer on layer, on its denial, that our only way into it is through destroying, in the name of all our culture, and of our whole human habit, the real person. We thus create the symbol of the very thing we attempt to deny, the symbol of man consummated in death.

The cross is not the negation of culture. The cross is culture's negation of God, of total truth, of total reality, this negation seen in a healing symbol. The only redemption of consciousness lies in the discovery that at the limit of its claim to constitute the absolute world it creates the symbol of what that claim denies: man perfected in death.

The cross is the one totally realistic dialogue between the man God made us and the man we make ourselves. The realism of the dialogue demands violence – the full operation of man's resistance – and its victim. It is our victim, and he alone, who opens up to us the death in which we are to find ourselves. There is too much in us that resists total truth, for us to come into that truth except via our

71

resistance. The mystic who flies in to this centre, must there look upon him whom he has pierced. He *has* pierced him, if he's a man, if he's concorporate with the human world. Remember the Christian tradition which says that I killed him, that my sins nailed him to the cross.

The cross is not God's denial of this world. It is this world's denial of God, the symbol of this denial which is the symbol of God's acceptance of this world. God so loved the world that he sent his only son. Any ascetical doctrine which sees in the cross the symbol of contempt for the world is a perversion of Christianity. For all its thoroughness in self-denial, it avoids that *central* self-denial which identifies with the crucifying world and allows God to show to man his sin and God's forgiveness. It assumes prematurely the stance of God, and so never meets him in his mystery of love.

Part Three

IN PRACTICE

1 SORROW IS ESCHATOLOGICAL

What is the essence of sorrow?

It relates in the first place to evil or harm done, whether consciously or unconsciously. Further, while common sense wants to know how a person can be expected to be sorry for something he did not know he was inflicting, reflection shows that coming to know what one has been unknowingly doing to someone is *closer* to the essence of sorrow. I am speaking of the peculiar unconsciousness that is always an ingredient in human relations and that turns out to have been *itself* the infliction upon another person, not merely that which *allowed* the inflictor to cause pain.

Another thing to be said of sorrow is that it is different from regret. For true sorrow requires total acceptance of the new state of affairs revealed when I become conscious of what I have been doing. It requires that I live, wholly and without distraction, with the person I now see myself to be. And regret, however human and even inescapable, contains an element of playing the whole sequence through again in my mind, this time without the offense. So a *part* of my heart is trying to keep its innocence, like Conrad's Jim, in 'Lord Jim', repeatedly acting-out in his imagination those fatal moments during which he made that cowardly leap into the life-boat, *this* time *not* leaping, *not* being the coward he now knew himself to be.

A third characteristic of sorrow is, that it can only come to full stature when the offended person is wholly forgiving. A person who is wholly sorry is, to a degree far beyond the normal, self-exposed. For such self-exposure to be met with 'well, we'll say no more about it', is degrading. A person who is wholly sorry is, by that fact, on for a dangerously new degree of intimacy. For this to be met by the other person out of the perfunctory resources of the earlier relationship, is for the primary human offense, that of being unconscious, to shift

74

from the offending to the offended person. It is a terrible thing to ex-act as payment what is being freely given out of a broken heart, thus showing oneself unworthy of the penitence of one's friends. On the other hand, the undivided forgiveness called for by undivided sorrow has more in it of the divine than of the human. To err is human, to forgive divine. It is significant that Shakespeare turns, in his most mature play, to the theme of forgiveness, *and* that he makes his mer-ciful character a quasi-divine figure.

What lies at the heart of this sorrow, that sees evil in a past ex-perienced as innocent, that would not undo that past, and that needs for its climate an unreserved forgiveness? What is this sorrow that is not so much *over* the past as *of* the present? What is this sorrow that is an awakening of the heart yet has for its appropriate symbol the broken heart? What is this *change* of heart that is rather the *discovery* of the heart?

This sorrow is an awakening; that is, an enlargement of the pre-sent and a new promise for the future. Yet the past, while it does not call the penitent *back* to itself, is essential. Imagine David's tears before Nathan without an intense reliving of his treatment of Uriah the Hittite. The thing to hold onto here is the concept of the past's *reviving* in the present.

How then are we to represent the three dimensions, of past, pre-sent, and future, as they interrelate in the coming of sorrow?

Contrast this process with our normal passage out of the past, in the present, into the future. Of the normal passage we are largely unconscious. We know the past as a situation that no longer prevails or applies, the present as a new call on our energies, and the future as the vague direction of our desire. Whereas in the process we are analysing, the past is turning into the present, and the present open-ing upon a real and significant future, *in the consciousness of the person.* The *person* is growing, and *that* is his experience of time. He *is* a becoming. An innocent and unconscious past *is becoming* a conscious present that asks what is now the work of love.

And this leads us to the crucial question. In this awakening of a once-unconscious evil to itself, in what is that evil now seen to have consisted? There is only one possible answer. My past evil is seen as my *suppression* of the self, of the true centre, that is now awakening. Not you my friend, and not God, but my true self, is the victim of what I now know as sin. I hurt you, yes. I failed God, yes. But more

75

radically than this and by a secret action that is the mystery of evil at its core, I rendered unable for you, unabundant towards you, and impervious to the voice of the Spirit and of life, that centre, that heart, whence alone human goodness can come.

It is my heart that my friend wants and that God calls upon. And a colloquial description is content to say that evil consists in *not giving* my heart. But the mystery of iniquity is that I may easily, and without infringing any commandment but rather allowing myself to be a decent average representative of my society, make it to be the case that I do not have a heart to give.

Scripture refers to sin as hardness of heart. But we need to ask *how* we harden our hearts. The trouble is that we confine our analysis to the human refusal in its practical effects – the gift refused, the attention not given – and so do not attend to the hardening of the heart. So we say that the sinner *has* a hard heart. His centre, we say, *has become* hard. And so we fail to see the subtler point that the centre as such cannot be hard. It can only be suppressed or, to change the metaphor, encased. We get so used to regarding the hard heart as *the source* of evil actions that we become incapable of seeing that the heart is the evil man's *victim*.

Now to this analysis of sin and its coming into sorrow, there corresponds that deepest analysis that is the centre of the New Testament. At least, a correspondence appears once we allow ourselves – with more theological tradition behind us than might at first appear – to see in Jesus the symbol of the true self. Jesus is, most intimately and without the aid of any vague pious rhetoric, the victim of sin, because he is the symbol of the true self, of that which we allow evil in us to neglect, ignore, and crush. His is the heart that I have refused to myself, to you, and to God.

I believe that a new hermeneutic of the doctrine of the Sacred Heart would surprise us. It would show the unimaginable extent to which evil, in God's perspective, is *man's* crucifixion. It could well be that the revelation to Margaret Mary was prophetic of, looked forward to, a newly internal understanding of theology. The vision is of an *inward* betrayal, and an inward healing: of the divine heart that man must eventually recognize as his own, wounded by the normal cultured life of man. This sorrow is the pangs of new birth. The essential pain of this new birth is indivisibly the pain in the heart of Christ and in the hearts of his awakening members. That which a person *becomes* in Christ is that which he *destroyed* in Christ: his ultimate identity, his freedom for God, his true self.

At the level of symbolism, there is a 'family likeness', a suggested connection – suppressed at the cost of maiming the symbolism – between the piercing of Christ's heart with the spear and the 'compunction of the heart' that is central to Christian mystical tradition. Compunction of the heart is more than the *resultant* of contemplating the heart of Christ. It is the entering into that contemplation; the *becoming* of what is *seen*; the putting-on of the crucified; the patterning-on the crucified. There is a middle term that holds together the piercing of Christ's heart and the allowing *my* heart to be 'pierced': that term is sin's piercing of my heart, become a consciously appropriated act. The faithful vision of Christ's heart pierced allows me to experience my heart as sin's victim and as taking to itself the penitent ego in a new life.

It is not pious consideration that breaks the sinner's heart. It is his vision of it broken by sin and awakening to new life as the breaking action is appropriated. What lies at the heart of this vision of the Sacred Heart is nothing less than the ultimate confrontation, essential to Paul's epistle to the Romans, between 'sin', the universal, culture-shaping nonpersonhood, and 'life', the life that God sowed on this planet with the birth of consciousness and looked to for his undivided praise and glory. The theatre of that confrontation is the heart of man, finding at last its true reflection in the Crucified.

The strongest theological minds have avoided this vision, relegating it to the pious, who see the Sacred Heart as human only in the sense of being God's way of bringing home to us the enormity of sin as offense against *him*. It enables us to see sin as hurting God. But God is all truth. The way he brings a truth home to us is itself the truth. What is brought home to us by the vision of the Sacred Heart is that sin offends God by destroying man, and that sin is redeemed in the resurrection of man.

St Bernard says that the most mature love is to love oneself for God. It follows that the most mature form of sorrow is sorrow over the unique life that I have made unavailable for the Spirit and for my brother. *Such* sorrow is, indivisibly, the awakening of that unique life to God and to his world of people. It is the tears through which a man comes anew to his God, to his wife, to his friends, to life. And since it is in Christ that a person becomes mature to God and to his world, it must follow that Christ *is* that life which he has killed and repents of killing.

A further step, hinted at already, is to say that unconsciousness not only *permits* sin but *is* sin. It is far clearer that it is *I* that am the victim of my unconsciousness than that I am the victim of what my unconsciousness has allowed me to do. That to which the crucified holds up the mirror is that in our normal living which has no place for, and sees no need to find a place for, our unique, hungry, humanity. It is that which will ask 'when did we see you hungry?' And of what will a man more innocently and self-righteously ask that question than of his own neglected life? The crucified enables me to see the self I destroy in the self I neglect. He enables me to see that to neglect *is* to destroy. And so I come before the crucified *as a non-person*, seeking to be awoken to the person I am. From him I learn that at my most innocent I am death-dealing. I come to him to learn the vertiginous leap from the man I have made of myself into the man I have in this self-making destroyed. Indeed the reason why theology has become so myopic is that we have lost the blazing contrast between God-made man and man-made man. We no longer hear, as pointing to the forgotten reaches of ourselves, 'Behold the Man!' We have very little sense of as lost, that which the Son of Man came to seek and to save. We do not recognize him dying on the Hill.

Nevertheless, what the Christian tradition has failed to see *intensively* in a single vision, it has *assembled*, piece by piece. It is in no doubt that the man born at Calvary is an unimaginably new man, his climate not the man-made city of historical man but the new eon of God. But it has failed to realise that the roots of this new way of being human must lie buried within the person we think we are. And so it has failed to appreciate that the crucifixion that is the threshold between the two worlds is that which crucifies, by its very normality and self-acceptance in a man-made universe, the heart that God has made and looks to for his praise and glory: our own. In considering the passage from the old world to the new, theology tends to look at Jesus' death not *as inflicted* but simply as the passage from one world to another that death may easily be thought of as being. I often find myself asking: wouldn't this theology work just as well if Jesus had died, with heroic patience, of lung cancer?

The turning-point is sorrow. And this sorrow, standing as it does between two worlds of man, the old and the new, is of more-than-man over less-than-man. It is of the more-than-man who appropriates all the evil in the world that makes us less than man, that crucifies in us the Lord of the coming glory.

In sum. That which makes of Christian sorrow an eschatological reality, the hinge between man-time and God-time, is the unity between the piercing of the heart of Christ and the compunction of the heart of man.

2   THE BUDDHA AND THE CHRIST

Gautama, who became the Buddha, came to think that desire is the cause of all suffering. Therefore eliminate desire, and you will come to peace.

This analysis does not go to the root of the matter. The cause of our unpeace and unfreedom is not desire by itself but desire mixed with fear.

Desire is basic. To be alive is to desire. But no sooner is desire conceived than fear says 'where will you be if you don't get what you want?' A marriage is thus formed between desire and fear. It seems a natural, even an inevitable partnership. For what more natural spur to desire could there be than the fear of not getting what I want? But the fear of not getting something is a motivation quite different from its desirability.

Normally we don't notice this difference. Desire as we experience it is clandestinely married to fear, very often even *directed* by fear. I spoke of fear as a *spur* to desire. Desire is the horse, fear the rider that has gotten onto its back. The horse is a good horse, and, liberated from this dark rider, will bound for the heart of the sun.

Let me give some examples of this confusion of desire by fear. A woman can make a man think he is in love with her – and vice versa – by making him jealous of somebody else. What is happening in the experience of the victim? 'Something I might miss' has, imperceptibly, become 'something I want'. The most potent advertising involves this same manipulation of desire through fear. The centre of persuasion is not the desirable object – the automobile, the after-shave – but 'you *without* these things, you bereft, you impoverished'. It is not appetite but ego that is the target of the advertising industry.

In these instances we can spot the connivance of fear with desire, the self-insinuation of fear into desire. But experience teaches that only the Holy Spirit can bring us to that deep place in ourselves where fear and desire combine, and dissolve this enslaving marriage. Even the Buddha, it seems, did not find that deep place: he *only* knew desire confused by fear. And so the only solution available to him was: eliminate desire.

Our lifelong task is to cooperate with God's gracious action of liberating from fear our desire for fulfilment. That is why, at every serious crisis of spiritual growth, we hear again the voice of fear: 'where will *I* be? What will become of me?' The art of spiritual discernment is to get to know that voice and to meet it with the question: what do I lack when I am free?

The contrast between the Buddhist and the Christian diagnosis of the human ill is essentially the same as the contrast between the sub-Christian and the Christian understanding of the cross. In the sub-Christian understanding, life is the crucifier, the ego the crucified. In exactly the same way, for the Buddhist analysis life is the crucifier, desire is the crucifier, the ego the victim. The Buddhist remedy is to eliminate desire, the crucifier. The Christian remedy is to realize that desire is not the crucifier but the crucified – by the ego with its characteristic climate of fear. Our human eros is manhandled in a thousand ways, misdirected, distorted, disguised, and eventually rendered hateful to us, by the fear that dogs it. And God's sublime remedy for this ill is the symbol of the true self and eros of man as victim, calling us not to the extinction of desire but to sorrow and a second birth.

I have learned this by experience, which is the only school. I can be crucified by a close relationship – driven out of my wits. But the moment of resolution and of light and freedom comes when I perceive that the inflicting element is not the love but *my expectations* of the person: my expectations, which are powered by a horror of the void, and set the person up as the filling of my emptiness. Of this ego-feeling, the love is the victim: not vice versa. The pain involved in accepting and following this insight can be intense. But it is a pain that is incredibly different from what we normally experience as the pain of desire.

3 A PARABLE OF FORGIVENESS

Let us look at the parable of the servant who, having been forgiven an enormous debt by his master, refused to remit a much smaller debt of his fellow-servant.

The truth this parable is getting at in its deceptively simple fairy-story way is the existential truth that lies at the heart of the human condition: that my hardness of heart in respect of my brother *disguises from me* the fact that I am enormously in God's debt. Instead of saying '*although* I have been let off a huge debt, I won't even let someone else off a small one', I should say '*because* I see no reason to remit my brother's debt, the forgiveness of God has no serious meaning for me.'

This turns the whole thing upside down. Far from my refusal to remit being manifestly outrageous to me in the light of God's forgiveness of me, it is my refusal that is preventing the light from getting through.

At the fairy-tale level, the refusal of the servant incurs severe punishment from the master. But at the existential level, the punishment incurred by our hardness of heart is the punishment *of not seeing* that we are in God's debt and in need of his forgiveness.

The parable taken simply as it stands is a description of the way it *objectively* is between man and God and between man and his fellow-man. It is not, *as it stands,* a description of man's *consciousness* or unconsciousness of these relationships. And this is our concern. This we must explore if the gospel is to live for us. We have to think of God's forgiveness as a transformation of consciousness.

We then realize that the connection between God's forgiveness of us and our forgiveness of each other is *organic*. There is only one experience, of the heart liberated *from* sin *for* our fellow humans. And conversely, the condition of not appreciating myself as in need of the forgiveness of God, *is* the condition of automatically subjecting other people to myself in my thinking. The 'normality' of insisting on payment *is* the sense of myself as autonomous, and this is an estimate of myself in which the forgiveness of God has no place.

The more we concentrate on the question 'how, basically, do I see myself?' the more clear this organic oneness of forgiveness needed and forgiveness given to another becomes. If I know only one centre to my life – the ego with its multiple concerns – then I am at a centre that does not know the need to be forgiven and that finds it normal to exact payment in one form or another. Conversely, if the mysterious, innerly spatial, *other* centre is becoming reality for me, then my ego begins to be 'placed' in a spiritual universe that declares its need for God's pardon and the preposterousness of exacting payment from others.

It is in the pardon of God, become a need and a reality for me, that other people leap, in my mind, out of the enslaving categories, of enemy or of expected-from friend, into a new and spacious mental world. Does it need to be said that they will notice the difference: or that if they don't, I have been playing games with myself?

It is increasingly a fact of my experience that the deepest, most obscure and most unavowed obstacle to a total surrender to God's forgiveness lies in the way I look at other people, lies in the system, built up over the years, of expectations and evaluations and projections. Of this fact the gospel is the one faithful and unflinching reminder. That is why it is indivisibly the witness to the awful majesty of God and to the brother in need. Anyone who reduces either of these dimensions of the gospel to the other is still estranged from his true centre where alone Jesus speaks.

This would be clearer to us if we understood better the relationship between attitude and action. It is simplistic to regard our basic attitude as the 'profound' thing, and action as merely symptomatic. As deeply as we *experience* ourselves, we *enact* ourselves. Our ill lies as deeply in the human world we *make* as it lies in the seeds of our motivation. This is why the gospel places the remedy of our ill in the acted-out condition of man the crucifier of life.

There is another place where Jesus uses the down-to-earth image of debt and payment. In the incident of the sinful woman at Simon the Pharisee's house, he tells the story of the two debtors, and concludes 'much has been forgiven her because she has loved much.' It is not that the woman, being a prostitute, had incurred a larger debt in respect of God than had the punctilious pharisee. Rather, the extent to which she has entered into the divine realm of forgiveness is *symbolised* by saying 'she has been let off a bigger debt.' The extravagant behaviour of the lover, contrasted with the correct behaviour of the normal pious person, has the privilege of opening up the *true* dimension of man, in which he owes millions to a God who happily cancels the debt. The man in whose self-estimate 'little has been forgiven' is a man who has as yet seen little of himself.

It is significant that it is this incident that produces the teasing and paradoxical saying 'much has been forgiven her because she has loved much.' The reason is that here the relationship between divine forgiveness and human behaviour has 'come off', whereas in the story of the servant it does not come off. It is where the forgiveness of God becomes human fact that we are plunged in paradoxical language and invited to correlate the bizarre behaviour of an immoral woman at a dinner party with the remission of an enormous debt on God's bank.

The idea of the divine forgiveness of sin is the most spiritually ambitious of religious ideas, and therefore imposes the greatest labour
on him who would make it his own. It conjoins the two extremes of
human experience: the infinite, all-transcending whole, and a man's
most particular experience of his own life as sordid, trivial, and
self-seeking. It conjoins the ultimately sublime with what Becker
refers to: 'Everything painful and sobering in what psychoanalytic
genius and religious genius have discovered about man revolves
around the terror of admitting what one is doing to earn his self-
esteem.' ('The Denial of Death' p.6)

Many today experience no difficulty in finding meaning in, and
desiring for themselves, God's forgiveness of sin. But generally these
people evince no sense of the *oddness* of this idea, of the disparateness
of the experiences which it bridges. The God whose forgiveness they
seek is a God whom traditional religion has for long *associated* with
the mental world in which sins are committed. In Freudian terms,
this God is the superego minus the latter's merciless rigidity. It is
altogether a different matter to connect one's personal sense of
meanness, the small mental world of which sin is precisely the
creating, with the idea of a centre of reality indifferent to what we are
immemorially habituated to regard as important: the Narcissistic
self of man, the 'real' centre of custom, of society, of philosophy, of
art, of science. To think of *such* a reality as 'forgiving sin' is mind-
taxing to the limit, possibly, of mind-destruction.

Now what I am beginning to experience *this* forgiveness as doing,
is going to work not on 'my sins' but on the way in which I *consider
myself* as sinful. This *natural* sense of sin is the revulsion at myself that
arises in a context in which I am the centre of attention. Not revulsion *at* regarding myself as the centre, but rather the revulsion-com-

ponent, the emotionally negative component, *of* the sense of myself as the centre. *This sense* is not questioned by the natural sense of sin, which arises *within* it, as its negative component, as the self-disgust that is the negative mood of an inflated self-awareness. This self-disgust stands to an integral sense of sin as a hangover stands to a real growth out of alcoholism. And the divine forgiveness is a gracious disssolution of that *system* of self-awareness in which I show up alternately as euphoric and depressed. It touches not the self-important sinner but the sin of self-importance.

In touching *this* sin, the divine forgiveness is *not* acting out of character with its infinite and beyond-me root. On the contrary, self--importance is *properly* dissolved by that infinite and luminous centre that is its ultimate corrective. What is meant by the divine forgiveness of sin is that God begins to be God in the small, mean life of the sinner.

And this touch of grace, for all that it is in character with its transcendent origin, enters most intimately into the small world of the sinner. It is dissolving that world. It is not ignoring it, or sweeping it aside, or urging me to forget about myself in my Narcissistic wriggle. It is getting into the wriggle, liberating the latter's captive. It is teaching me to experience myself in all the sordid particular of my life of sin, but with a strange difference. I am being taught to experience all my meanness in a new context. In this learning, I become more not less aware of the meanness. I am invited to contemplate 'what I am doing to secure my self-esteem.' The divine forgiveness of sin is the gracious presence of a new context for my meanness to experience itself in. Its roots are at the luminous unseen heart of the galaxies: its presence is in my sordid particular.

And as this discovery proceeds, I begin to see my meanness as a *making*-mean what is in itself not mean. Let me illustrate this. A friend seeks my advice on a recent interchange with a person, in which he obscurely feels he has been obtuse. I point out to him where I think he might have overlooked something. Immediately he says 'O I'm always doing that. You're so right.' No good has come of the dialogue thus far. He has merely swung from the 'euphoric' position, in which he has done the damage, to the 'depressed' position, in which he 'always behaves that way'. And, incredibly, this swing to a blanket self-denigration is an almost unconscious ruse on his part to *avoid* the truth I want him to look at.

In a moment of light, I might be able to make him see that what is at the root of a bad relationship with others is something he is doing to himself, is a real potential that he is destroying. The thing we most need to be told, and most resist being told, concerning an experience when we know we have been at fault, is how good we basically and potentially are. Nothing hurts so much as having one's own individual, unique life touched, with its freedom, its responsibility, its unknowing.

Thus to come into the transcendent forgiveness situation is to re-experience my meanness in a new context that breaks it down into 'something I am doing to myself'. 'Myself, alternately experienced as pleasing and revolting' gives way to 'something I am doing to myself'. And this internal action in its turn gives way to the beginning of a dialogue. 'Something I am *doing* to myself' turns into a dialogue that I am *having* with myself.

Now it is with the coming of this interior dialogue that the forgiveness situation begins. For now there is awakening within me, as the victim of my meanness, as the bearer of my own life, the spark of true being that belongs in the totality of being. That which awakens, in a new sorrow and beyond praise and blame, is *my life*, my freedom to be, my responsibility to existence. I begin to be able to think of myself, in my meanness, as touched by the God who is the live centre of all being. Far from forgiveness being something the believer seeks from a God already defined by his religion-culture as the forgiver of sin, the very *idea* of forgiveness is experienced as the bridge between the human meanness, normally interpreted in an ego-centred way, and the transcendent centre.

The self that I am repressing, immobilizing, alternately enjoying and blaming is the self that demands, in its brittle fragility, the worship of other people. In the critical instance of a grave offense from one of the worshippers, this self assumes its extreme posture of self-securing: the unforgiving posture. In other words, having analyzed the self-immobilising, self-securing position, we have to look at this as it relates to other people. And there we find a continuum, of which the unforgiving situation is only the extremity. *Along* this continuum we encounter the more normal situation in which the captive self imprisons others in the categories of 'objects of our expectation'. Even before they are judged unforgivable, they are extensions of my system of self-esteem. And this system, which totally breaks down when I receive the grace to forgive an enemy, already is trembling in the balance when I understand that my expectations of others are stemming from what I am doing to myself.

Now we are at the point at which the opening of a person to God's forgiveness, and the yielding of that person's basic stance in respect of others, may be experienced and understood as one same breaking-down of the normal system of self-esteem and self-denigration. To forgive an enemy is to risk my whole system. To open myself to the forgiveness of God is to risk my whole system. It is the same risk. And Jesus' insistence on the forgiveness of enemies, as though that were the whole substance of salvation, is based on a perception of this identity in the risk. He is saying 'take the risk there' – where the presence of another human being, selfish and mean like yourself, precludes any possibility of bullshit. In that sense, to forgive one's enemy *is* the whole of salvation. If *that* is happening in a person's life, the forgiveness of God is happening in its primary meaning.

We can therefore paraphrase 'Forgive us our offenses as we forgive those who have offended us' thus: 'Grant us to experience that true divine forgiveness whose working in us is the dissolution of our normal unforgiving system'. 'Forgive us our sins, *in the way of* us forgiving each other.' 'Forgive us our sins *as* 'us forgiving each other' – that is to say, truly.' It must have struck many people that there is something odd about this petition. We couldn't be asking God to model and measure his forgiveness of us by the forgiveness we manage to accord, sometimes through clenched teeth, to each other. And yet the forgiveness of man by man *is*, in the *wording* of the prayer, the model. 'As we forgive'. The only resolution of this problem is to say that God's forgiveness is pictured in *that* inter-human forgiveness that is its mirror-image, a mirror-image that only appears in human experience when the central light has come on, when God has made himself known to us in the forgiveness of sin. 'Forgive us our sins so we can see it, live it, in a new community.'

The gospel has received two different descriptions. One runs: 'The gospel is the proclamation of God's gratuitous forgiveness, a forgiveness apprehended in faith and expressed in sacrament.' The other runs: 'The gospel is the one really radical ethic, based on the forgiveness of our enemies.' There is no disjunction here. The first is the transcendental analytic description, the second the existential. Both are contained in the statement that the gospel is the one definitive statement on the forgiveness of sin. The gospel is doing two complementary things. It is presenting a *real* idea of God's forgiveness, as opposed to the idea that we form in the attempt to placate a God of our making. And it is presenting a *real* idea of the forgiveness of man by man, as opposed to the forgiveness we sometimes just find a corner for in our immemorial and acculturated egoism. The normal idea of God's forgiveness and the normal idea of human forgiveness belong to and express one system of human self-estimation with the ego at the centre, having God as its chaplain and the suitably repentant enemy as its beneficiary. Corresponding- ly the real idea of God's forgiveness and the real idea of human forgiveness belong to and express the system of the new man in critical and penitent and growing dialogue with himself.

Finally, the divine forgiveness that works itself out at the heart of man's meanness has for its all-powerful and all-gathering symbol the Man on the Cross. For that symbol tells us that sin is the destruction of the good that is in us. It takes us beyond the cop-out whereby we compensate a euphoric self-esteem with self-denigra- tion, into the dialogue between the crucifier and the crucified that is at the heart of every man. And in the final analysis, the sorrow that is the place of all forgiveness is not even the sorrow of the crucifier but the sorrow of the crucified. I believe that the well-spring of con- version, perhaps only discerned later when the conversion situation has matured, is that which belongs to the true God-implanted self of man as he awakes on the cross where sin has placed him. The heart of Christian sorrow is the Man of Sorrows.

When one person forgives another, the change happens in the forgiving person. We say that he 'relents', abandons his uptight stance. But when God forgives, it is the forgiven person's heart that is changed. Human forgiveness is the unhardening of the heart of the pardoner: divine forgiveness is the unhardening of the heart of the pardoned.

This contrast is the basis of the connection between being forgiven by God and 'forgiving one's brother from the heart'. For in the case of God's forgiveness, the *essence* of being forgiven is the unhardening of the heart, which is the *essence* of forgiveness of a man by another. That which *originates* human forgiveness, the unhardening of the heart, is *originated* by divine forgiveness.

If we ignore this difference between divine and human forgiving, we are confined to saying: 'you have been forgiven (by God): therefore you *in your turn* should forgive your brother.'

But if we confine ourselves to this human model, we have to consider that though the relenting takes place in the pardoner, he who receives pardon only truly does so by allowing his heart to be changed. The real fault of the servant in the parable consists not in refusing forgiveness to his fellow-servant, but in not appreciating the forgiveness he has received. To be forgiven is to be set free: which should raise the question 'free for what?' Certainly not to continue one's tyranny over others.

While the forgiveness of a man can be received without appreciation – as the immense relief of being able to cancel that ugly figure in one's balance sheet – the divine forgivenesss cannot be received *at all* without appreciation. Appreciation is its substance. The changing of the heart is its substance. And of that substance we must give, or eliminate it from our experience. The divine forgiveness either creates a community or it is not received.

6 PERSONAL EXPERIENCE AND PAUL

The following experience led to the formulation of the principle of inversion which is central to this book's theme. I was giving a course of lectures which, so far as I could judge, were going very well. One day a close friend asked me 'how was this morning's class?' 'Good', I replied, 'they're really the best lot I've had'. He replied that he had overheard a few members of the class saying they hadn't a clue where I was going and were very frustrated. I went to my room, and sat like a stone. Although I had a talk to give in an hour, I could not turn my mind to it. I was dead, destroyed, and angry.

After about half an hour I thought vaguely of the cross and the new thoughts I was beginning to have about it. In connection with the painful experience I had just had, I began to ask 'what's going on here?' *Somehow* the suggestion then formed itself (and not in answer to the question 'who's crucifying whom?', because that question only came into my system *as a result* of this experience) that, contrary to my *feeling* of being crucified by my friend's information, it was my ego, with its inveterate euphoria, that was the crucifier, the class – or rather the true situation between the class and myself – the crucified. Euphoria is a great destroyer of life with its vast variety of tones and shades. It will have everything to be going splendidly – or else it will resign. Meanwhile life is trying to breathe. This student has understood. That one has not. That other one thinks he has, and has understood something else. And so on. But the ego will have none of this. And its first target – though not easily spotted – is my self, my body, the actual communications that are going out to those men and women.

With this thought I began to revive, with a new feeling for my class, for myself, and for life. In an hour I knew that I had made a for me very important discovery.

I see now what Paul means by crucifying the flesh. The flesh is the ego. Yet I have argued that the ego is never crucified, only *thinks* of itself as crucified until I discover the true cross in a situation. In spite of appearances and immediate reaction, the ego is crucifier. But *then* I have to identify with the crucified part, with the truth, with my true self. And *this* move is death to the ego, and *then* life to me who am thus freed from the ego's tyranny.

To crucify the ego is not to act against it. To crucify the ego's lusts is not to repress them. It is to put the ego on that cross *that itself is inflicting*, and thus to undergo death in the ego, or death as far as the ego is concerned, and so to find life in the crucified self.

The Pauline askesis of crucifying the ego-flesh, once it is grasped, opens the door to the following Pauline description of the new condition of man in Christ Jesus. 'When anyone is united to Christ, there is a new world; the old order has gone, and a new order has already begun.' (2 Cor. 5, 17). The newness consists in the fact that a person who finds himself in Christ goes through a door on the other side of which everything is reversed. The basis of this reversal is the reversal of the ego's version of crucified and crucifier: the follow-through is the self-identification with the crucified in the particular situation, which means death to the ego and a new flourishing of the person's real being. This death to the ego, death to the ego in this Spirit-directed and wholly creative process, is 'mortification'. We do not hear this word any more. In the period immediately preceding its demise, it had come to mean a dreary sort of emotional hari-kari, and as such was then rejected on the time-honoured principle: first play the tune wrong, then stop playing it altogether. In the meantime, breezy, well-intentioned spirits say that all Paul is talking about is self-discipline, so let's call it that instead of 'mortification'. This is not what Paul is talking about. He is talking about the mystery of the crucified as it daily enlarges our lives in freeing us of our ego-illusions. Far from being an emotional hari-kari, mortification is an emotional liberation, turning the energy that we expend in unconsciously strangling our life into the freeing of it.

We can then understand the numberless texts in which Paul describes the new life as freed from sin. The fact that this freeing process has to be gone through again and again as our ever-changing life meets new challenges does not alter the fact that structurally, and each time it happens, the liberation is definitive, an end and a beginning. The Christian life is not a continual struggle against sin in which sin *gradually* yields to grace. It is the process of repeated appropriation, in ever new circumstances, of a *total* and definitive ending of sin and beginning of life. The process viewed over a timespan is of course gradual. But in its interior, it is rather a series of quantum leaps, each leap being constituted by a death of the ego-flesh. The heart of the process is the each-time total death and unpowering of the ego, rendered possible by the self-manifestation of the crucified as the structure of the believing heart: by the presence, that is, of the self as the crucified, in whose favour the ego is called on to surrender.

It is fatally easy to impose on Paul's exposition the principles of a common sense askesis of struggle against bad habits. Surely these are what Paul means by sin. And of course the converted have resolved to struggle against it. They decree an end to sin simply as a person does when he makes a good resolution. Obviously that's what Paul is talking about! But it's not what Paul says. This common sense understanding ignores Paul's statement 'sin has *died* in you'. Paul's charge against his Corinthian converts was not that they weren't keeping up the struggle against bad habits, but that they weren't letting Christ work in them, that they didn't realize what had happened to them, what they had in them, what they had it in them to become. Nor do we.

Liberation from sin is rooted in the *forgiveness* of sin only when sin is understood as the tyranny of self-worship, revealed in Christ as at root self-crucifixion, and resolved in the faithful vision of the crucified. In this ultimate form of forgiveness, in which *God* forgives, it is in the forgiven person, not in the pardoner, that 'relenting' happens. Thus the freedom which, in an interpersonal situation, is generally experienced more by the forgiver than the forgiven, in the divine forgiveness is wholly in the forgiven. We are let off from worshipping ourselves. God lets us off from worshipping ourselves, and so frees us for life.

Thus we have two choices for our understanding of Paul: a holistic interpretation and a common sense interpretation. In the common sense interpretation, sin has its common meaning. God has forgiven our sins – by some wonderful arrangement he's made with Christ. But sin still stays with us – 'the one that got away', or our bad habits – for us to struggle with. There's no connection between God's forgiveness and this continued affair with sin. God's forgiveness does not mean the end of sin *in us*, except as perhaps inspiring a good resolution. In the holistic interpretation, God in Christ has revealed the root of sin in us as self-crucifixion, and so enabled us to experience his forgiveness as the liberation of us from ourselves, a liberation which we enjoy anew each time we find the cross in our lives, identify with the crucified, and so let the ego die. In this view, forgiveness equals liberation, and liberation powers the ongoing askesis. Thus the Christian life is simply the prolongation of God's forgiveness of man in Christ.

CHRISTIAN SELF-DISCOVERY
A paper read at the Lonergan Workshop, Boston College, U.S.A., 1976

The thought of Bernard Lonergan centres on the most important fact about the human subject. Among the continually expanding number of facts about this most complex and intriguing being, the most important is, that he is self-transcending. All the writing of Lonergan is, in one way or another, heading the reader towards the recognition of this fact *about himself*. Self-transcendence is personally discovered to be the case, or it is not properly understood. And into this discovery one is dragged, protesting, kicking and screaming. For on the journey inward towards this recognition – for which the Augustinian word confession is the most appropriate – one travels through all sorts of subsidiary systems of oneself, each deploying its own characteristic distracting virtuosity and complaining against a threatened takeover. The struggle is similar to the Ignatian journey towards a devastatingly honest and grace-enabled self-appraisal, which also is a journey through protests – styles of living, slowly assembled and established to meet life's challenges as best one could, protest that life on any terms other than theirs is simply impossible. At the end of both journeys – or better, of both modalities of the one journey – the self that is revealed as *my* self, and that can no more be doubted than I can doubt that I exist, is a lover, is generous, finds peace in the other, lives in a limitless universe, is self-transcending.

Self-transcendence, then, is not a property to be attributed to a being called 'man.' It is something to be discovered about myself. It is something that *is* discovered in so far as I discover myself. The discovery of the self carries the discovery of self-transcendence within it. The correct assertion 'man is self-transcending' invites us first to conceive, somehow, of a being called man, and *then* to *add*, as a notion distinct from the notion of this being, that it is self-transcending.

But the discovery I am speaking of works differently. In it, the notion of self-transcendence is not *added*, but grows out of the self as freshly appropriated and acknowledged – grows out of as the only way I can henceforth understand or speak about myself. What is absolutely essential to the discovery is that the intimacy, the I-ness, of the self, has self-transcendence as its structure: that the realization 'that is I,' with all its undeniable sense of homecoming and a huge familiarity, invokes love as its meaning. 'I am' equals 'I love.' 'I love' is the only way to say 'I am.'

But this discovery is not made by 'going into oneself.' St Teresa does talk sometimes about 'going into oneself,' but this phrase is, for her, only a sometimes appropriate shorthand for what she does in contemplative prayer. It is only the self as realized in some great and mysterious adventure that reveals, as its deepest secret, that it is lover. The obstacles to true self-discovery are many, formidable, tortuous and perverse. They are only cleared through some unaccountable generosity that can occur in the very thick of our total involvement with others and with the God who queers our pitch with others and with ourselves until we accept the grace to let him speak. In what follows, I want to examine the most intense and crucial of all our involvements: the situation of offense, of hurt, of forgiveness, of reconciliation, and, finally, of that human guilt which, beyond the reach of even the most loving and patient of friends, eats away the self and challenges an infinite love to dissolve it. It is in a true and accurate assessment of this situation above all that we may hope to discern that the human subject is indeed lover. The battle-scarred being who in this most human of all situations eventually opens his eyes and smiles, is a self-entangled lover. The skilled love that seeks him out seeks *that* in him: for that is who he is. A forgiveness that does not believe *that* of him is no forgiveness and will only compound the misery.

I have been led to this theme by a class-room experience of the last semester. Teaching theology to freshmen and sophomores who only come to me in the fetters of 'the Theology Requirement,' I found that an extensive and sophisticated analysis of the structure of forgiveness between people awoke much interest and solicited some remarkable end-of-term papers. From this I came to two conclusions: that forgiveness, and all that it involves and all that involves it, are the things that interest God most; and that the things that interest God most are the things people are most interested in. The first conclusion comes as the end of a persistent meandering study of the gospel that has to be measured in decades. The second, though crashingly obvious, has taken and is taking courage to implement.

My treatment falls into five sections:

1.   A human forgiveness situation. Its implication is: that the hurt we deliver is at root our self-hatred, the suppression of the lover in us. So forgiveness is only *received* through, or in, or as fostering, self-acceptance.

2.   Having considered the *interpersonal* situation of forgiveness, I zero in on the *forgiven subject*. How does *he* stand in relation to his fault? I find that, integral to his reception of forgiveness, integral to his revival as lover, is a very accurate, free, and full admission of his fault. And for this to be possible, he must have an extraordinary confidence in being accepted. Jesus understands this structure, operative between people, as the very structure of the soul and involved in its ultimate healing. So the theme of this section is Jesus' treatment of sinners as described in the gospel.

3.   I find that, grounding and profoundly enriching the gospel concept of sinfulness is the concept, wrestled with by Paul, of enmity with God. So correspondingly, grounding and profoundly enriching the gospel concept of forgiveness, is the Pauline concept of reconciliation. This is the full meaning of our acceptance: the release from enmity, the release of the lover.

4.   I ask the deepest question: what is it in us that radically inhibits belief that we are accepted? This brings us to a guilt that precedes and exceeds the moral sphere. The theme of this section is the full and final confrontation between Jesus and the sinner: the cross and the resurrection.

5.   Finally I discern a need to correlate this *generic guilt*, from which the gospel exonerates us, with the *sins* of which we are justly ashamed.

1.   The structure of forgiveness

What happens when Mary, who loves John, forgives him for an injury he has done her? What is involved, in her and in him, in this transaction?

On her side, she continues to love him, and to let him know it, not primarily in words but in the wordless way that is open to lovers.

On his side, he 'hears' from her that she still loves him. So he 'hears' from her that he is still lovable, still of value. But at the same time, he is experiencing himself *not* as of value, but as having treated someone badly.

Thus her love is setting up a contradiction, in him, between 'I am good' and 'I am bad.'

The only resolution of this contradiction is for him to see that in hurting her he is hurting himself. This resolves the contradiction, for it makes John's badness consist in attacking, striking at, his own goodness. I can be, at one and the same time, good and bad, *if* my badness consists in the suppression of my goodness.

Now this is precisely what her love is telling him: that what he takes to be badness in himself is the suppression of his goodness. It is *not* that he is 'no good.'

This brings us to the most important thing about true forgiveness: namely, it is the opposite of what we normally think forgiveness is. The normal understanding of 'being forgiven' is 'I am bad, *but* you forgive me.' I *am* no good, but *even so,* you're *so* good that you forgive me. Whereas true forgiveness means Mary reawakening John's sense of *his own* goodness which has taken a big knock from the way he's treated Mary. True forgiveness is love in action awakening the offender to the good he suppressed *in himself* in hitting out at the offended one.

The point is, that when I have hurt someone, the easy and natural way for me to level with that fact is to regard myself as a lousy no-good person. My pride prefers to keep it that way. That is why it so often happens, when someone has hurt another, that he *keeps repeating* 'I'm just a selfish bastard, what else can you expect?' This *sounds* as though he's admitting his fault, being very humble, taking the blame. But *really* he's using these words *in order to* stop her forgiving love from getting to him. He doesn't want to hear that he is good in this situation that he can only level with by thinking of himself as bad. He prefers not to face the *full* situation, which is that he has hurt another person *by shrinking himself.* When you hurt another person, your true self, the lover in you, goes into hiding, and uses every possible ruse to stay in hiding. Even abject apology!

So the full experience of being forgiven is, *first of all*, the experience of a sharp contrast between 'being an offender' (being offensive) and 'failing myself,' and *then* the invitation to *move* from the first self-description (as offensive) to the second (as failing myself). Above all, the experience is a poignant sense of the love (Mary's) that is enabling one to make this rather amazing move. For Mary's love is essential here. If John, without considering her at all, says 'all that's happened is that I failed to live up to my full potential,' he is an impossibly smug person.

In sum, true forgiveness does not merely 'forgive the offender.' It awakens him to his true being that he rejected in being an offender. It restores to the offender the dignity of being a self-forgetful lover. Forgiveness is a restoration to the self, and is the climate in which the *meaning* of the self has its clearest radiance.

2. Concentrating on the subject of forgiveness, the forgiven subject.

When we concentrate on the forgiven subject, we encounter a paradox. While it is an obsession with how bad he had been that inhibits his reception of forgiveness, it is also the case that a person can only fully confess to his fault when he is certain of receiving it. I cannot admit that I have done wrong; I cannot admit that I have made a huge mistake, except to someone who I know accepts me. The person who cannot admit that he is wrong is desperately insecure. At root he does not feel accepted, and so he represses his guilt, he covers his tracks. And so we get the paradox: confession of fault means a good self-concept. Repression of fault means a bad self-concept.

Jesus understood, as no one else has at such depth and with such simplicity, that this simple fact *between* people manifests something in the very structure of the soul. He knew that a person's deepest insecurity is caused by a sense of guilt accompanied with no sense of being accepted. He found a way to open people's eyes to themselves as accepted by God, so that they could, in the serene confidence of this acceptance, confess their sins. He went further, in that he brought people to an act of confession that was *itself* the supreme act of confidence in God's acceptance. In this way he brought about the greatest spiritual revolution that ever occurred. Religious man had done *everything* with guilt except totally acknowledge it. Jesus enabled man to do just this. He made this possible by enabling him to feel accepted in his very being. At a hitherto unknown level of acceptance and confession, he lifted definitively the burden of guilt that, at

99

every other level, man can only shift around. He actualized, between man and his Maker, the structure of admission-in-acceptance that we discover between ourselves. We have yet to bring this structure down to its deepest level of operation. This must wait until we consider 'generic guilt.'

This is the logic of the gospel concept of sin and forgiveness. The consciousness of sin that Jesus awakens in people is something completely new in the history of religion. The newness consists in being enabled to say 'I have sinned' in the way a man can sometimes say 'I am sorry' to his wife or his friend: namely, in a way that gives expression to his utter certainty of being accepted. The gospel confession of sin is the most generous, secure, adventurous expression of the human heart. It is the risk that is only taken in the certainty of being acceptable and accepted. It is the full and final expression of that confidence. Only to your lover do you expose your worst. To an amazed world, Jesus presents a God who calls for this confession only so that he may reveal himself in a person's depths as his lover. This confession in a context of divine acceptance releases the deepest energies of the human spirit, and constitutes the gospel revolution in its essence.

The most important characters in the gospel drama are those 'publicans and sinners' we have heard about since our Christian childhood. They are important because they most clearly illustrate *that* consciousness of sin which cripples the spirit. They are the people whom society has told they are bad. Their sense of guilt has eaten into their very identity therefore, and made them unacceptable to themselves or to anybody else. Jesus awakens in them a sense of acceptance, so that they can acknowledge their sin in the certainty of being accepted. He does not say 'society says you are doing wrong but I say you are not.' Prostitution and the rip-off of the tax-collectors is a destructive way of life, and Jesus knows this. What he says is 'you can acknowledge your wrongdoing in a way that exposes you to the acceptance of God.'

'It was said to them of old "Thou shalt not commit adultery," but I say that anyone who looks on a woman with lust has already committed adultery with her in his heart.' The intention behind this statement is to bring good people who would stop short of adultery to recognize the sin that is in us all and that now at last can find confession and acceptance. It is to promote good people to the status of sinners, who can *then* be promoted to the status of unfaithful lovers. Robert Frost has expressed this well (in *'A Mask of Mercy'*):

> Christ came to introduce a break with logic
> That made all other outrage seem as child's play:
> The Mercy on the Sin against the Sermon.
> Strange no one ever thought of it before Him.
> 'Twas lovely and its origin was love.

He goes on to explain that curious phrase 'The Mercy on the Sin against the Sermon.'

> Paul's constant theme. The Sermon on the Mount
> Is just a frame-up to insure the failure
> Of all of us, so all of us will be
> Thrown prostrate at the Mercy Seat for Mercy.

This is perhaps the place to remark that the gospel exposure of the roots of sin in the heart is ruinous outside the context of divine acceptance in which alone Jesus makes this exposure. You then get what Francois Mauriac, in 'La Pharisienne,' called 'the Furies of the New Covenant.'

Let us now return to the basic logic of the gospel of forgiveness. It is, I have indicated, paradoxical. The paradox may be expressed thus:

> Admission of fault = a good self-concept
> Repression of fault = a bad self-concept

Unfortunately, the Christian tradition has screwed up this paradox. By the way in which teachers talk about sin, the 'equals' signs have got misplaced thus:

> Admission of fault ✳ a good self-concept
> Repression of fault ✳ a bad self-concept

Thus the admission of fault runs 'I am a miserable sinner, a no-good bastard.' And conversely, the only 'good self-concept' that the teachers recognized and correctly upbraided is the smug self-satisfaction obtained by repressing fault. So the 'equals' signs go diagonally across the diagram.

The task of rectifying this error is immense. It means learning to read the gospel without hearing its words on the 'tapes' of centuries of Christian programming. 'God will forgive you, but first you must confess your sin.' Isn't that what the gospel says? Yes, but the meaning is 'confess your sin so that God can reveal himself to your heart as your lover and friend and so your heart can come alive again, the lover in you can be reborn.'

It has taken me thirty years to understand that the admission and forgiveness of sin is the essence of the New Testament. The recovery of this truth is seriously compromised by centuries of misunderstanding. For it is the delicate operation of recovering this truth from the well-meaning people who, repelled by the negative understanding of it, have placed the essence somewhere else. This complex error must be redeemed if we are ever to feel again the magic of Jesus which promotes 'man the sinner' to the dignity of man the unfaithful lover.

3. Enmity with God and reconciliation.

We've already said a good deal about God. We bounced off the John and Mary story pretty freely, and likened God's forgiveness of the sinner to Mary's forgiveness of John. And then, in the second section, we said that the dependence of confession on acceptance works with God as well as with each other. But now we've got to deal fairly and squarely with the fact that God isn't a bit like Mary or anyone else: for the simple reason that we can't see him or touch him or hear him or experience him in the way that one person experiences another. We may say, as Jesus does in effect say, that God's attitude to us is one of acceptance, as Mary's is in our story, but how do we *experience* God as behaving towards us in this way?

There's a real problem here, and for God's sake let's recognise it, otherwise we shall never appreciate the deep mystical dimension of God's love. The problem shows up once we recognise the crucial difference between *saying* that God behaves like the Father of the Prodigal Son, and *mediating*, making available, this behaviour of God. The bright kid in the religion lesson appreciates that the appearing of God at the level of *meanings* does not tell us whether God *is* or is a Father. He's onto the same thing. The *likening* of God to the forgiving person John experiences in Mary is not the *making available* of God to our experience as one who loves and liberates.

I have said that God is quite unlike Mary in that he is not visible or tangible or audible or kissable. Now this *cause* of unlikeness, this *ratio* of his unlikeness, is *per se* a theme for *mistrust* rather than trust. Heavily prejudiced already in the direction of non-self-acceptance, we are to that extent in need of visible and tangible support, and this is precisely what we don't get from an invisible, intangible God. So his absence makes him suspect at the soul's gut-level where assurance is so desperately sought for and where even the goodness of friends is often unavailing.

This basic existential mistrust of God underlies all historical religion, though it is not avowed. Let's look at historical religion for a moment. By religion I mean simply the *existential* negotiation of God as opposed to the purely *cognitive*. Now I suppose that there are two ingredients in man's religious negotiation of God. One is, of course, man's self-transcendence, the yearning of his spirit for the All. But there is another ingredient which really contradicts the first, and actively inhibits its flowering, in other words inhibits recognition of God as the all-originating love-energy by man the lover. This other ingredient is constituted not by *wonder* at our being but by an acute *unhappiness* with it, a sense of worthlessness, of insignificance. With this 'wretched' creature man, with this self-fulfilling prophecy of failure, God is *contrasted*. This is one of the great Old Testament themes: the power, the splendour, the holiness, the sublimity of God, as against this worm that is man.

Now there *is* of course a contrast between the infinite and the finite, but *motivating* the contrast is a sense of worthlessness. The God who is so great is the God who regards *us* as nothing. At the limit, God becomes the very name for our worthlessness, the Ultimate Reality whose non-acceptance of us confirms our suspicion that we are not acceptable. Thus pushed to the limit, the God-of-the-sense-of-worthlessness is the exact opposite to the God-of-the-sense-of-self-transcendence and, if allowed to, would blot him out.

It never comes to that of course. Though note the savage cruelty and self-destructiveness of much pagan religious practice. And for that matter, look at the God of Jung's 'Answer to Job'.

Now the God Jesus is talking about is a God who is experienced *only* through the sense of self-transcendence and *not at all* through the sense of worthlessness. And this is a God *never heard of before*, for the simple reason that never before Jesus was there a *man* totally without the sense of worthlessness.

We are going to see later how Jesus gets this nearly impossible message through to us. Suffice it to say here that once the message *had* got through, Paul could cry out 'My God, don't think, you people, that we *loved* God! We hated him! Tell it like it is. Now that we are reborn we see in retrospect with what resentment our sense of worthlessness took it out on God, though of course we always kept religious good manners. Now at last we are *reconciled* to him. Yes, reconciliation is of *us* to *God,* not of God to us.'

The end of the story is that man the lover is completely vindicated, justified, acquitted. And that's what the love of God is. This is the Resurrection, the hatching of man the lover out of the thick milennial cocoon of man the sinner. How, at the climax of the story, Jesus becomes man the sinner, will be the theme of the next section.

4.   Generic guilt

> Do I dare
> Disturb the universe?
>
> T. S. Eliot, Prufrock

Now at last I've got to think about guilt. I need to get a *generic* notion of guilt, some idea of its general shape before it enters into all the distinctions such as that between neurotic guilt and reasonably acknowledged guilt. What is guilt, most generally conceived? What, generically, occasions it?

It is very closely associated with freedom. The girl who decides to leave home feels guilt, mainly perhaps because of her mother. The child who plays with another child of whom his parents do not approve, or who even *thinks* otherwise than his parents about this matter of friends, feels guilty. And the great myth of the Fall, that dominates the Christian tradition, presents guilt as arising, as it were automatically and in the nature of things, when the man and the woman make a bid for independent judgment, for making the world their world, its good and evil their good and evil.

In other words guilt seems to be the accusation of some enclosing whole or order against one who breaks out from it. 'How could you

104

do this to us?' asks the family, or the religious order, or – more radically – the psychic womb. The all-pervading, all-beautifying world of 'participation mystique' cries out in gentle outrage and pain against the newly self-aware and self-disposing. How could you do this to us? Now you are alone. How will you be without our comfort? Now you are forlorn, with only yourself to consult. Where will you go? What comfort can you now find within your independent existence, you who but yesterday fed sleepily at the breast of an all-embracing life-power?

Guilt, then, is the accusation that freedom draws from the psychic womb whence it breaks out. It grows with consciousness itself. More accurately, it grows with self-consciousness. That independent self which begins to sally forth in this world carries, from the very start, a baggage of accusations from the blissful world of unconscious childhood. 'You're on your own now!'

Thus guilt, in its most radical form, is not generated by the non-conformity of my action with the relevant social mores. It inheres in my action precisely as a free, as opposed to a 'being-part-of' action. Its gravamen is not non-conformity but independence. It is hardly distinguishable from loneliness.

Now the next thing to consider is how a person *handles* this inbuilt accusation. He is not, and it seems he cannot be, untouched by it. What I think we do is, that we allow to the accusation its description of what we are doing, and say 'hell I'm going ahead in any case.' We consent to be *guiltily* on our own, *guiltily* about our own business. We *accept* the psychic womb's description of our independence as 'filthy.' I believe that the note of *defilement* that Ricoeur finds to be absolutely fundamental to the notion of evil, arises precisely at this point. The contrast between what ridiculous, pretentious, independent little 'I' generates and this huge enclosing world of earth and sky is one in which I appear dirty. With my individual mark I deface the universe. Whence, for instance, came the idea, so easily ridiculed by liberals, that sex was 'dirty'? Was it simply the geographical proximity and in part identity between its organs and the organs of excretion? Surely no, the 'dirty' bit got in with the 'mine alone' bit, and inextricably mixed up with it. A man or a woman, in almost every known culture, hides his or her sex organs not, I suspect, because they are sex organs but because they are *his* or *hers*. They are even *called* 'private parts.' And it may be that sexuality is, of all areas

105

of human experience and experiment, the most guilt-ridden precisely because here we have the most dramatic conjunction of the universal life-force (the psychic womb bit) with the mine and the yours of the self-conscious, self-emancipating individual. Human sexuality is the dramatic breach with the life-force, the defacement of the universe by conscious people. It is a use of the impersonal life-force that is highly personal, original, adventurous, bizarre, perverse, beautiful.

In summary, guilt is 'the human animal persisting in what the psychic womb accuses him of: accepting the latter's description of what he is doing, and doing it none the less.' We see then how closely guilt is involved with freedom.

These two elements: the acceptance by our freedom of our earlier world's disapproving description of it, and the persistence in our independence under this description, form, with the accusation itself, the structure of guilt. Accusation, acknowledgment, and persistence. We carry into our new world of freedom the accusations of the old world that bore and nurtured us.

'What are *you* doing?' says the universe to this upstart man. 'Why did you do that?' asks the nun of the child. 'Because I wanted to.' 'Do you *always* do what you want to?' Into the very heart of individual conscious action there is injected that note of privacy, of theft, of cornering something off for oneself, which is sounded off by 'the whole.' And when the family or the religious community accuses the one who leaves it, it is this archetypal structure that is operating. The community's protest and the resultant painful interchange constitute the diachronic dimension. The structure of accusation, acknowledgment and persistence constitute the synchronic dimension.

'It goes a good deal deeper than what people call their conscience' says Harry in Eliot's play 'The Family Reunion.' 'It is rather the canker that eats away the self.' The guilt with which the human race has to deal is far more than the memory of heinous deeds. It is the coloration of human self-conscious activity by an indignant cosmos. And whether or not a person does things that can rationally be judged to be bad, his primal sense of guilt precedes and itself colours these doings. Thus another may forgive him for them. But his forgiveness will come up against the *core* sense of guilt and there founder.

And this last consideration takes us an important step further on our enquiry. If *I*, conscious I, am somehow against the whole: if I am my own doing: if I am stolen from the whole: if I am this private thing of my own inventing: if I am a defilement, a defacing mark: *how can I be acceptable*? How can I be welcomed into the whole whence I have cut myself off, whence I *am* the cutting-off? The problem of the forgiveness of sin is at root the problem of the *acceptance* of the forgiveness of sin: which is what Tillich calls the acceptance of acceptance. It is terribly hard to accept the embrace in a heart that has grown solitary. The difficulty of a middle-aged bachelor in coming into love is one diachronic enactment of the synchronic structure that we have now built up into a fourfold structure: accusation, acknowledgment, persistence, and then non-expectation of acceptance.

Christian belief places at the climax of its story a man without sin. Does this mean that Jesus was without *guilt*, without that generic guilt of which I have spoken, which seems to be an inalienable part of the coming of individual consciousness? And if so, what are we to make of the consciousness of Jesus? On my showing at least, human consciousness without guilt is hardly conceivable. At least we may not draw on any examples from our experience or from history or from literature. (And least of all, be it noted, the experience of saints.) But then this mystifying quality, in such a Jesus, of *consciousness without guilt*, is balanced or complemented by another quality, equally mystifying, of intimacy with the Absolute which, most would I think agree, appears to differ qualitatively from the religious experience of all the other great religious leaders. In other words the absence in Jesus of self-securing against the whole is one side of a coin of which the other is a total certainty of *acceptance* by the whole. And this, it hardly needs saying, not in the manner of the happy pre-conscious animal. Jesus is not pre-Adamic man. He belongs to the future rather than to the past.

Out of this consciousness Jesus proclaims, and cannot but proclaim, the universal forgiveness of sin. In a consciousness that knows nothing of 'acknowledged rejection,' he knows a God who accepts. He proclaims this God as one who always forgives. The source and matrix of the Christian conviction of God's forgiving love is the guiltless consciousness of Jesus. Thus 'the God and Father of our Lord Jesus Christ' and 'the Lover of all' are *conceptually* identical.

God's unique presence to Jesus is the ground of his proclamation of God's forgiveness.

But the interaction between people and the phenomenon of a guiltless accepter of acceptance would be complex. For one who is free of guilt altogether, free even of the generic guilt, will be a terrible accusation to me. He will make me conscious of the guilt in my whole build-up as a person. In his presence, my life is undone. Layer by layer, the assemblage in guilty independence is exposed. I am bewildered by the terrible presence of an alternative to what has seemed to me and to everyone else to be the only way to live, the only way to become. And yet the whole *message* of this presence is, that the *accusation* of the psychic womb against my freedom *has no claim on me,* that the self-conscious life which contracted this stigma is in reality the most beautiful thing in the cosmos and most acceptable to God and accepted by him. This dismantling of my life effected by the presence of Jesus is only what is produced by the searching fingers of love. But can *I* feel it this way? Can I sense the fingers of love? No, at first it is the threat that I feel.

And so we get a paradox. The *presence* of the guiltless one accuses my guilt, awakens guilt long forgotten and indeed hardly perceived as guilt: while the *message* of the guiltless one is precisely that I am *not* guilty, that the charge against my freedom was falsely pressed and mistakenly accepted.

There is no resolution of this paradox at the level at which it occurs. For guilt, as I have analysed it, is the very cement of my building. Totally without it, totally deprived of my private self-affirming, I would fall apart, I would die. The only resolution is for him to undergo the death that I would die if I could accept his message of acceptance by God. *He* must die the death of the old world. *He* must fall apart. The love with which he offers man the sinner God's acceptance must turn back on him as death.

And thus we begin to understand those features of the Pauline soteriology that are the deepest, the hardest, the hardest to understand, and the most easily misunderstood. These are: 1. Jesus' death as substitutionary, 2. the strong statement that 'God made him to be sin for us,' 3. the image of Jesus as embodiment of the old Israel that had to die for God to appear.

We seem to have grasped the crucial point at which our guilt is transferred to Jesus. It is the logic that makes the bearer of the Good

News its first victim: the victim in whom we find our peace.

It is in the death of Jesus that our perception of him as accusation dissolves into the true perception of him as the sign of our acceptance. For, as we have seen, it is his death that resolves the paradox which held his message of acceptance trapped in the form of accusation.

But it is only in the experience of Jesus as risen that this new perception can come to us. For the risen life of Jesus means this: that the death that is the only way out from the paradox of divine acceptance of man the acceptance-repeller leads into the true life of man as the accepted of God.

It is not just death that is crowned with resurrection. It is the death of the old man. It is the death that God's acceptance seems to involve to the guilty freedom of man, and that is accepted by the proclaimer of this acceptance. It is the violent death that is the second name of the sinless proclaimer of God's acceptance of sinners. For it should not need saying that the synchronic structure that entails the transfer of death-inviting guilt from us to Jesus is worked out diachronically as the violence that comes from the interpretation of love as accusation. We kill 'our accuser.' In the resurrection we encounter 'our lover.'

It begins to be clear to me that the blood of the cross flows, symbolically, from a life assembled with guilt, that guilt which is the oldest ingredient in what we know as self-conscious man. For it is at the *generic* level that the structure of 'accusation, acknowledgment, persistence, non-expectation of acceptance' is assembled: whose dismantling is the Passion and Death of the Lord: whose total alternative is the Resurrection.

Note

The main contention of this section is that moral guilt is not the adequate category for understanding the gospel of redemption. For this understanding we need to consider that more radical guilt which virtually equates with loneliness or forlornness and which excludes, or rather repels, divine acceptance. It is something very underattended to. I can only recall a few haunting sentences in Kierkegaard, and some fine observation in Eric Neumann's 'The Origins and History of Consciousness.' It also occurs to me that Scheler's 'ressentiment,' surely the most horrible observation ever achieved by a philosopher, is the reaction of generic guilt to the freedom of another . . . .*

5. Guilt and sin

> It is really harder to believe in murder
> Than to believe in cancer. Cancer is here:
> The lump, the dull pain, the occasional sickness:
> Murder a reversal of sleep and waking.
> Murder was there. Your ordinary murderer
> Regards himself as an innocent victim.
> To himself he is still what he used to be
> Or what he would be. He cannot realize
> That everything is irrevocable,
> The past unredeemable. But cancer, now,
> That is something real.
>
> T. S. Eliot, The Family Reunion

I have spoken of our 'generic guilt,' as something that comes into being with our freedom: a heard accusation on the part of the psychic womb as it parts to let us out. I have said that this has to be distinguished from sin, in that it is characterised by independence rather than by transgression. But now we have to see how this generic guilt, while distinct from sin, relates to it.

First let us define sin. This is an exercise of our independence in a way that injures another person or society. Now the relationship between generic guilt and sin consists in this: that the already present sense of being guiltily on my own makes the sinful act something that 'comes naturally' to me. I am already this private being: so why not go all the way with this 'me-for-me' condition? The act of sin does not appear *to me* in its stark destructiveness. I do not see it primarily in the context of the order with which it breaks. I feel it as a natural emanation of my privacy. Its context is my atmosphere as a private being, in which it fits, not the order that it disrupts. Or – what comes to the same thing – the order itself is seen rather as that primitive enclosing order, the psychic womb, with which I *have* to break in order to realize my freedom at all.

Footnote: Scheler's book is called simply "Ressentiment".

110

Van Breeman, in 'As Bread that is Broken,' has a brilliant analysis of the sin of David over Bathsheba. The affair starts with David, the extroverted warrior, who is hot and can't sleep. There's nothing wrong with that, says Van Breemen. Of course there isn't. It is ordinary consciousness. And it is the sense of me-for-me. It is the guilty privacy of an ordinary man. But it will be the justifying base for all that follows. For next comes the sight of the girl bathing. (Well, I'm a man aren't I, and a king to boot!). And so one thing leads to another. The adultery is beautiful. In David's consciousness, it represents the original 'me-for-me' now broadened out into a river of delight. Thus the original justifying context is enlarged. So enlarged, so beautiful, so engulfing, that it makes natural the summoning of Uriah back from the front to give David a first-hand account of how the campaign is going. Then the attempt to get Uriah to sleep with his wife, and, when this fails, the expanded plot of David's inner drama makes natural the plan to eliminate Uriah, involving Joab and an unwarranted tactical risk. Joab foresees that the soldier in David will be angry at this needless risk until he hears that Uriah has been killed. And so it turns out.

So enmeshed is David's whole act, for David, in the original self-justifying context, that the prophet Nathan has to use an indirect method to fish it out from this subjective sea and present it in all its enormity as getting a man killed in order to get his wife. He tells the story of the rich man plundering the poor man of his one lamb. In that figure, David is presented with an act of sin *without* its subjective justifying context, and he positively shakes with moral indignation. Then he is caught, for Nathan has only to say 'that man is you.'

What I want to emphasize here is David's justifying context. And what I want to suggest is that this justifying context justifies *because* it is itself a guilty state in the generic sense of guilty. Somewhere inside is the little voice that says 'well, you're on your own you know . . .' It is this sense of being somehow originally outlawed that, albeit very inexplicit, grounds our evil deeds, and, when they come, gives them growing and beauty in our eyes. The self that I *consult*, when I proceed to what is possibly a very wicked deed, is *already* 'offside and content to be so.' Thus the generic guilt that, contrasted with adultery and murder, must be judged innocent, *drawn into consultation* becomes a principal actor in the drama.

Moralists have always been intrigued and puzzled by the small beginnings of big sins. But they easily miss the point here, and describe the small beginnings as a 'proneness to evil,' and warn us to watch out for 'our sinful nature' in its very earliest stirrings. There is of course a practical common sense at work here. Still, the point is missed. For the point is only grasped by attending to the puzzling character of the process. The point is that we *find ourselves* doing harm, rather than initiating the harmful act in a clear way. St. Paul says precisely this, in one passage that everyone remembers because it is so astonishingly rare of its kind in moral literature. And we puzzle ourselves in doing harm because of that peculiar base in consciousness from which we operate: precisely because, I mean, there's no harm *in the base itself*, yet it has limitless power to justify evil actions, or at least to keep them soft in our eyes. It's really got us foxed, this bipolar structure of 'innocent guilt' and sinful act.

Nor is this to mitigate or to soften the evil in sin. Quite the contrary, it is to bring our attention to the real nature of sin, which lies not in 'rebellion against God' but in the peculiar dialogue of alienated man with himself. Sin is the sealing of alienation, its total normalizing. Hannah Arendt's phrase 'the banality of evil,' fearlessly used in connection with the concentration camps which less morally perceptive people can only describe with superlatives of malevolence, is entirely apposite here. The Godlessness of man is not rebellion against God but, just what the word says, God-less-ness. It is that peculiar me-for-me condition in which alone freedom can get going. It is the human beginning-without-God, the consideration of which generates the paradox of a God who apparently creates man to fall and be redeemed.

The error of the 'moralists' referred to consists in understanding the base (generic guilt) in terms of the evil deed, instead of the other way round. They stretch the evil deed back, back, back, to a sort of mini-evil-deed, a homunculus of evil, instead of grappling, as a few do, with the puzzling nature of the base, that tantalizing quazi-equation of guilt with loneliness. Of course the 'other way round' is much more difficult to handle. But only so can we open up the ethical picture to its theological dimension.

But there is a vital further step to this argument. That very guilt which let sin come easily and legitimates it in our consciousness, is what generates the feeling that there can be no radical forgiveness. The very on-my-own-ness that I consult to ease my way into sin will be my unavowed reason for hoping for no forgiveness. I may *say* 'How can I be forgiven for this murder?', but what I am really saying is 'How can *I*, who do a thing like that, be forgiven?' What I am really looking at is not simply the murder but the murder *coloured* by my guilty self-awareness. A person's sins become for him an enlarged version of an original loneliness. Originally, the sin hid in the generic guilt. Now the generic guilt hides in the sin and makes of the latter a typical manifestation of my lonely, estranged self. Thus the original justifier of sin becomes its accuser.

But its accuser in a half-hearted way. For as long as I feel unforgivable I am still clinging to my sin *as* a typical manifestation of myself. I am still *colouring* it with my lonely selfhood. And *that* means that I am not fully *acknowledging* my sin. Strange as it may seem, there is a difference between saying 'Good God, *I* did *that*' and saying 'Of course I did that, what else can you expect?' What is strange is that it is the former that is the real confession of sin and not the latter, in spite of the latter's apparently greater humility. The latter way of speaking is not a confession of sin but a posturing of 'the sinner.' And the real intention of this posturing is to maintain, as a kind of last-ditch defense, some of the *justifying* force of the generic guilt. People do this. They confess their sins orgiastically in order to maintain themselves in their proud and frightened solitude. And the capital point here is that the self is being kept in a state of osmosis with the original self-sense that is pervaded with the generic guilt. And this because the thing above all feared is the exposure of the self to the love that is the self's true climate.

That's what the gospel is about. What Jesus seeks in each of us is the frightened shivering creature which, before any of us can remember, huddled into the garment of guilt which the psychic womb wove for it as its only protection against the rude wind of an unknown love. The psychic womb is the God who sewed those leaves together to hide our first identity. The gospel is going back to that beginning of us, and calling us out into our end.

In short, the sourse of sin in us is not a homunculus of evil in us: it is a lonely frightened being whom the cosmos has chased into the isolation that we know as man.

Thus our analysis brings us to the most radical understanding of the self, to the confession of what Eliot calls, 'the essential sickness and strength of the human soul.' I am, in my deepest identity, self-transcending. I deny myself, and therefore God, in saying that I am on my own. This denial is the human guilt that only an incomprehensible love can dissolve. It is done incomprehensibly on a gibbet. Imprisoned by guilt, I am liberated by love. Guilt *is* imprisonment. I am that extraordinary creature, of whom love, coming to me and awoken in me, is the purging. And only a relentlessly prosecuted understanding of the self as self-transcending can do justice to the existential identity of 'coming to me' and 'awoken in me' and to the labour of this redeeming.

Epilogue

My epilogue is the description of a prayer in which this whole drama of the self is enacted. It is taken from 'The Last Western' by Thomas S. Klies, being the description of 'The Listening Prayer' as practised by The Silent Servants of the Used, Abused, and Utterly Screwed-up.

It is of the essence of the listening prayer that the listener put himself away from the pleas and suggestions of the normal self, especially when a life-giving action seems the recommended course, for the normal self will suggest many false deeds for the sake of pride or guilt removal or vengeance or for the satisfaction of desires that go back to the time before love spoke.

In all true listening the listener opens his spirit to the Loving One, the Power and the Strength as some call Him-Her, the YOU, who is wholly Other and yet also wedded to the true self. And it is of the essence and perfection of true listening that once the demands of the normal self have been completely put aside, the voice of the self wedded to Truth and Love speak in such a way to the heart of the listener that he is assured it is not other than the voice of the Loving One Him-Herself. And the listener knows this with the exact same degree of certainty that he knows that he exists.

Gloss of Marion Byrne: Has nothing to do with the lying and insanity of hearing voices, as the Fools of Spain believed. Entirely a matter of opening self completely to Other so that Other might enter and be joined to self so that when self speaks, it is the Other speaking in true wedlock, with utter clarity even though the language may be obscure to the normal self and even unknown to the mental workings of the normal self.

In any situation where the sacrifice of one's own life is required, one realizes it with a serene joy and absolute confidence because the road is so clearly marked, and there is never any doubt. If there is hesitation or confusion, the purest listening is required.

Explanatory note

Some definition of 'the lover' is called for. I would suggest: the lover is one whose well-being consists, and is experienced as consisting, in willing the well-being of another. Now there are many experiences to which normal usage would accord the name of love, that do not answer to the above definition. The heavily romantic form of love for instance. Nevertheless, these experiences, though they don't fit my definition, are judged by it and found wanting. The romantic lover has not yet discovered what love is all about. And this means he has not yet discovered how *he* loves. 'How I love' and 'who I am' are one identical discovery. He has not yet discovered *himself* in the act of loving. For him the act of loving is an act of self-forgetfulness, of in-attention, of chosen dreaming. In other words, the condition of willing another's flourishing is precisely a condition in which I am newly in touch with myself. 'Newly' is vague. The change is crucial. The new self-awareness is revelatory.

Thus the Goldsmith* progression: through the five stages of affectivity ending with the agapic is precisely the process of coming to myself, of the emergence of the real self into conscious volition and control. It is the progress of myself as lover through the necessary confusions and dead-ends to clarity. In the same way, progress in prayer, according to Abbot Chapman, passes through desiring to will what God wills to willing what God wills. The desire is already controlled, confusedly (and how confusedly! almost imperceptibly) by the emergent will whose 'successful' operation, it is already very dimly perceived, is to move in harmony with the transcendent and all-controlling will.

There is a section-heading in Austin Farrer's difficult book 'Finite and Infinite' called 'Will the clue to the nature of desire.' This has always fascinated me. I felt that I knew and did not know what it meant. That meaning is now clear. Desire cannot make ultimate sense as 'desire for something.' It is desire for a subjective condition:

*From as yet unpublished notes by Charles Goldsmith, Ph.D.

and the subjective condition is 'willing,' and willing, unlike desire which is for that which is not, is of that which is, independently of myself. To that happy condition, desire tends. From that happy condition, desire gets its nature and meaning.

Ignatius describes a condition of 'consolation without a cause.' It is for him an experience of grace. He says it can only come from God. My analysis of this condition would be, that in it I experience myself as happy precisely as willing. I experience will as the term or end of desire. In the customary order, desire explains willing, motivates the will, and happiness consists in having got, by willing, what I desired. In the deeper order that is here operative, happy willing seeks, and can receive, no explanation outside itself, no explanation in terms of something desired. Nor is this a question of some inner well-being or well-functioning operating in isolation. On the contrary, it is precisely the oneness of willing with attunement to an independent reality that is the substance of the delight. In this delight, will is *identified* as willing that which independently is, *I* am identified as willing that which is. In this experience I know myself as self-transcendent: and this is not a knowing something *about myself*; it is the knowing *of myself*.

In the experience of maturely loving another person, I am in touch with myself. But I cannot then say that apart from this experience I have no self, no being. There is still, for me, a substantial self, a principle of continuity that would continue to support me were this love to be no more. Whereas in the experience described by Ignatius, I know that 'outside this, I am nothing. Outside this, I am not.' In those privileged moments when the essence of willing is laid bare, I know that all-controlling, independent will, outside of which I have no being.

In the light of this clarification of my meaning as lover, I would say that the reason why the experience of radical forgiveness is crucial to our salvation is, that in this experience the step into the self's being as lover is taken in the only way that embraces the whole reality of our existential condition. All other steps into selfhood are short cuts. It is the self as immemorially pervaded by generic guilt that has to rise with Christ from the dead of sin.